The Ideal Woman

Elizabeth Mwachari

Scripture references taken from the King James Version,
The Amplified Bible, Zondervan Corporation and Lockman Foundation copyright © 1987,
The New Living Translation Bible by Illumina Gold Benny Hinn Edition by Tyndale House Publishers copyright © 2003

Copyright © 2007 Elizabeth Mwachari

All rights reserved. No part of this publication may be reproduced, stored in a retrieval system, or transmitted in any form or by any means, electronic, mechanical, photocopying, recording, or otherwise, without the prior written permission of the publisher.

ISBN: 978-1-60383-047-8

Published by:
Holy Fire Publishing
Unit 116
1525-D Old Trolley Rd.
Summerville, SC 29485

www.ChristianPublish.com

Cover Design: Jay Cookingham

Printed in the United States of America and the United Kingdom

Table Of Contents

INTRODUCTION 5

BACKGROUND 9

TREASURABLE VIRTUES 17

HERE SHE COMES AGAIN 28

THE REAL WOMAN 40

THE GOLDEN OPPORTUNITY 43

PRECIOUS VIRTUES 44

THE ULTIMATE RESULT 58

TO REVERENTLY AND WORSHIPFULLY FEAR THE LORD 59

THE WISDOM OF GOD 70

THE TREASURES OF WISDOM 87

A WOMAN IN GOD'S EYES 93

GOD GIVEN ROLES FOR A WOMAN 116

THE BEAUTY OF A WOMAN 120

THE PRINCIPAL THING 135

GIRL TALK 136

THIS IS WHO YOU ARE 140

IN CHRIST JESUS 140

INTRODUCTION

I would like to thank and appreciate the Lord Holy Spirit for helping me in writing this book to the glory of the name of my Lord and Savior Jesus Christ. I also thank my lovely husband Videlis for his encouragement and love while writing this book and also to my little boy John, God bless them both.

Being a wife and mother who loves the Lord Jesus Christ I started noticing that there is a need of mentorship for young mothers and younger women in the world today and as I read the bible I realized its biblical (Titus 2:3-4) to actually have older women teach and mentor younger women in life. That is when I asked the Lord and He gave me a desire to search the scriptures; by His tutelage the Lord Holy Spirit showed me that a real woman is not what the world says a woman is, but rather what the manufacturer Himself who is Jehovah God had in mind when he created a woman. There are ideal women in the bible, which reminds me that we are wonderfully and fearfully made with a purpose to fulfill on this earth. The bible says in the book of Ephesians that we are His handiwork (Ephesians 2:10) and this is what it says in the Amplified version of the Holy Bible: for we are God's [own] handiwork (His workmanship) recreated in Christ Jesus ,[born anew] that we may do those good works which God predestined (planned before hand) for us [taking paths which He prepared ahead of time], that we should walk in prearranged and made ready for us to live]. A question I always had was this; what is my purpose in life? Why was I born a Kenyan woman? Well I got the answer in the bible as you have also seen it in Ephesians chapter 2, the 10nth verse and found that I was created by God for a purpose which is to do good works like to teach other women through the leadership of the Lord Holy Spirit that women are the handiwork of the Lord God Almighty and there is a path he made for us women to walk in ahead of time(even before the world portrayed women as sex vessels being used to show off nudity) there is a good work waiting for women to do that the Lord God Himself predestined us as women for and not what the world says about us but what God says about us. Women are valuable in God's eyes otherwise why did He give us the mandate to bring forth human life? The world depends on women to populate the earth and nurture the next generation of human beings in this planet without women there is no procreation (think about that). Women are worth more than rubies and precious gems if they are in the Spirit and being led by Him. My passion is to let women know that we are precious and valuable in the eyes of our Lord Jesus Christ and not sex objects being used to gratify lustful eyes, I hope you know what I mean by that. So I trust the Lord that by reading this book all women will appreciate the privilege of being born a woman and do the good work that Christ has predestined us to do as ideal women of God. So I pray that as you read this book you will change lives of other women young and old. I am in my thirties now so I hope it will help younger women discover that they are originals and not counterfeits. My sister its God who designed you just as you are whatever you skin color may be or nationality, no matter your social status or age we are all one in the Spirit of God and God has a purpose for your life. I pray women will realize that it wasn't an accident that they were born female it was actually a privilege, reason being we are called into the helps ministry which to me is the most vital in life because even our Lord Jesus Christ told us that if we want to be great in this earth then we must serve others. Remember our Lord washed His disciples' feet He was in the helps ministry (John 13:1-17), so I encourage every woman who reads this book to take up the challenge and be an ideal woman.

There is one woman I will use to sight as an example but there are many ideal women in the bible like Esther,Hannah, Naomi, Ruth, Rahab, Mary the mother of our Lord, Dorcas the prophetess, Elizabeth the mother of John the Baptist, Sarah, Rebecca and many others. This book does not claim that the shunnamite woman is the only ideal woman in the bible, I was led by the Lord Holy Spirit to use her to site a few characteristics modern women need before we get to the bottom line of who is an ideal woman of God. God bless you as you read this book and I pray in the name of Jesus that it will change your life for ever and bring you closer to the heart of our Lord and savior Jesus Christ.

BY   ELIZABETH   MWACHARI

SHUNNEMITE WOMAN

BACKGROUND

This is a woman who is barren but is rich and influential, the husband now is old but she has this desire in her heart; to have a child; who wouldn't? If you are a mother, you can remember the joy of having a child. You and I know that children, that is biological children cannot be bought, you cannot give money in exchange for getting pregnant!!!

I don't know about you, but I really sympathize with this woman because I have been in situations in my life where only God could help; no amount of money could help and so I think I can identify with what she felt, do you? Have you ever been in a situation where only God could help not necessarily having a child but it could be something else like paying your rent, or paying off your mortgage or some bill? It could be an incurable disease maybe that has afflicted you or your loved one, those are many nowadays. If you have, then you can identify with what this woman went through. I can imagine talk from relatives especially the in laws!! And the pressure the man had to go through now that he was old and wealthy with no one to inherit!! Think of what his friends told him probably in some cultures he would be encouraged to marry a second wife who is more fertile! Remember there was no option to adopt as we are blessed to have nowadays. I think I have gotten you into her shoes by now!

But you know, God is so good and He gives us the desires of our heart (Palms 37:4) and He did, but read how the drama unfolded in 2Kings 4:8-36. God is good all the time; look at what He did for this woman, hallelujah!

2 Kings 4:8-37 (KJV)

And it fell on a day, that Elisha passed to Shunem, where was a great woman; and she constrained him to eat bread. And so it was, that as oft as he passed by, he turned in thither to eat bread. And she said unto her husband, Behold now, I perceive that this is an holy man of God, which passeth by us continually. Let us make a little chamber, I pray thee, on the wall; and let us set for him there a bed, and a table, and a stool, and a candlestick: and it shall be, when he cometh to us, that he shall turn in thither.

And it fell on a day, that he came thither, and he turned into the chamber, and lay there. And he said to Gehazi his servant, Call this Shunammite. And when he had called her, she stood before him. And he said unto him, Say now unto her, Behold, thou hast been careful for us with all this care; what is to be done for thee? wouldest thou be spoken for to the king, or to the captain of the host?

And she answered, I dwell among mine own people.

And he said, What then is to be done for her?

And Gehazi answered, Verily she hath no child, and her husband is old.

And he said, Call her. And when he had called her, she stood in the door. And he said, About this season, according to the time of life, thou shalt embrace a son.

And she said, Nay, my lord, thou man of God, do not lie unto thine handmaid.

And the woman conceived, and bare a son at that season that Elisha had said unto her, according to the time of life.

And when the child was grown, it fell on a day, that he went out to his father to the reapers. And he said unto his father, My head, my head.

And he said to a lad, Carry him to his mother.

And when he had taken him, and brought him to his mother, he sat on her knees till noon, and then died. And she went up, and laid him on the bed of the man of God, and shut the door upon him, and went out. And she called unto her husband, and said, Send me, I pray thee, one of the young men, and one of the asses, that I may run to the man of God, and come again.

And he said, Wherefore wilt thou go to him today? it is neither new moon, nor sabbath.

And she said, It shall be well.

Then she saddled an ass, and said to her servant, Drive, and go forward; slack not thy riding for me, except I bid thee.

So she went and came unto the man of God to mount Carmel. And it came to pass, when the man of God saw her afar off, that he said to Gehazi his servant, Behold, yonder is that Shunammite: run now, I pray thee, to meet her, and say unto her, Is it well with thee? is it well with thy husband? is it well with the child?

And she answered, It is well.

And when she came to the man of God to the hill, she caught him by the feet: but Gehazi came near to thrust her away. And the man of God said, Let her alone; for her soul is vexed within her: and the Lord hath hid it from me, and hath not told me.

Then she said, Did I desire a son of my lord? did I not say, Do not deceive me?

Then he said to Gehazi, Gird up thy loins, and take my staff in thine hand, and go thy way: if thou meet any man, salute him not; and if any salute thee, answer him not again: and lay my staff upon the face of the child.

And the mother of the child said, As the Lord liveth, and as thy soul liveth, I will not leave thee. And he arose, and followed her. And Gehazi passed on before them, and laid the staff upon the face of the child; but there was neither voice, nor hearing. Wherefore he went again to meet him, and told him, saying, The child is not awaked.

And when Elisha was come into the house, behold, the child was dead, and laid upon his bed. He went in therefore, and shut the door upon them twain, and prayed unto the Lord. And he went up, and lay upon the child, and put his mouth upon his mouth, and his eyes upon his eyes, and his hands upon his hands: and he stretched himself upon the child; and the flesh of the child waxed warm. Then he returned, and walked in the house to and fro; and went up, and stretched himself upon him: and the child sneezed seven times, and the child opened his eyes. And he called Gehazi, and said, Call this Shunammite. So he called her. And when she was come in unto him, he said, Take up thy son. Then she went in, and fell at his feet, and bowed herself to the ground, and took up her son, and went out.

Wow! What a story, but what is really behind these words that the Lord wrote, I believe the bible is just not filled with stories that mean nothing they mean a lot and so let us take it verse by verse and learn more about this woman. The first thing is this woman was wealthy and godly otherwise how did she notice that Elisha was a prophet? She must have been led by the Spirit of God to see something was different about this man, Elisha he was a man of God. And with that then if you let me talk to you a little then I will, not every bad thing in life that happens to us is to hurt us but it's to show forth the glory of God, why do I say that? Look this woman was barren with no child and the husband must have been very old for even Gehazi to have noticed that he was old and because of the biology of the activity of having children he couldn't make his wife pregnant. Notice another thing, the Lord wanted to bless this woman through the man of God but she didn't seem interested to get anything back for the hospitality she had shown the man of God. Remember even when the Lord Jesus sent his disciples to preach and told them to carry nothing with them in terms of money and supplies he told them whoever welcomed them they should leave the peace of God in other words the blessing of God with those who showed them hospitality. So in the same case here we see Elisha doing the same but the woman declines. As we always do have you ever been in a situation where you have given a gift or helped someone and then they ask if they could give you a thank you and you refused? I know I have lots of times done that. Well I think its time to learn how to receive when you give, it is a principle in the bible that if you give it shall be given back to you (Luke 6:38). But anyway she still receives because there was an obvious thing she lacked but was too ashamed to speak about or maybe she thought it was impossible so no one could solve that problem for her she had to live with it. Have you been there? I have. Where you think oh no this one I have to live with it. No, no you do not have to live with any problem or be ashamed to ask God for help. He is able to do exceedingly abundantly above all me and you can ever ask or even imagine! Oh yes God is able. There is nothing impossible to Him, hallelujah. Look at these verses with me please if you will;

Ephesians 3:20

Now unto him that is able to do exceeding abundantly above all that we ask or think, according to the power that worketh in us,

Luke 1:37

For with God nothing shall be impossible.

There is something the shunnemite woman did that we should be careful about, remember when the man of God told her what the Lord was going to do for her she said no. do you see that? This is something many people are used to today because of a lot of disbelief and also because when one is used to a problem that has been there for too long they tend to think its part of them and no one can alter that situation so they start talking disbelief even when God talks to them. Has that happened to you? I know of women who keep on speaking unbelief and so kill their miracles all the time. Watch what you say because the bible says in the book of proverbs that we shall eat the fruits of our mouths and also that the tongue has the power of life and death. Women talk a lot you know that is how we ventilate what is in our hearts! So my dear sisters have a look at these scriptures with me so that we do not repeat what the woman from shunem did;

Proverbs 13:2

A man shall eat good by the fruit of his mouth: but the soul of the transgressors shall eat violence.

Proverbs 18:21

Death and life are in the power of the tongue: and they that love it shall eat the fruit thereof.

These are good scriptures to help us learn to t~~~ and start speaking positively and good, edify~~~ situations, our children and husbands, ver~~~ amazing to me how such a story can help us ~ character; did you see how loving the Lord is and how w~~~ He is to give us the desires of our hearts? I hope you did but now lets us go step by step and identify a few more treasures of virtue that this godly woman had. I learnt if you read the bible and let the Word of God speak to you then it will help you change from one glory to another and so become a better person each time you read the Word of God. I pray that you will have a teachable spirit and get your bible, read with me this passage of scripture again and take this study with me please, would you?

TREASURABLE VIRTUES

From this woman's life drama, we as the 21st century women have a lot to learn from her so go with me, if you will through the word of the Lord, as we learn together how to be real women of God.

❖ She was hospitable

was a rich and influential woman who loved to host men God. I am sure that was a desire the Lord put in her heart and this was the way she served the Lord through the gift of being caring. We can say she wanted to facilitate prophet Elisha in his ministry so she wanted to be a willing partner of his ministry. This woman knew something most of her neighboring women didn't, that is; the Lord gives rewards to those who care for his servants and indeed He is a rewarder of those who diligently seek him.

Hebrews 11:6

But without faith it is impossible to please him: for he that cometh to God must believe that he is, and that he is a rewarder of them that diligently seek him.

❖ She was spiritual that is lead by the Holy Spirit

She could perceive by the Lord Holy Spirit that Elisha was a man of God and so she decided to up her stakes in her pursuit for God's favor in her life, she asked her husband if they could build the man of God a room to rest instead of just providing meals; in other words she increased her commitment as a ministry partner of prophet Elisha. This reminds me of a verse that says that the Lord's eyes go to and fro the whole earth and so He sees all we do [2 Chronicles 16:9 says; For the eyes of the LORD run to and fro throughout the whole earth, to show himself strong in the behalf of them whose heart is perfect toward him. Herein thou hast done foolishly: therefore from henceforth thou shalt have wars.] Just as Cornelius, this woman's deeds went before the Lord as a remembrance, this happened in the book of Acts chapter 10 and verse 4, it says; Cornelius stared at him in terror. "What is it, sir?" he asked the angel.

And the angel replied, "Your prayers and gifts to the poor have not gone unnoticed by God!

We serve a righteous GOD who never forgets our prayers and our giving, He will always notice what you do for Him, hallelujah!

So now the prophet gets a guest house to rest plus meals wow! Now this gets the prophet thinking what will he do for this woman? I get excited right at this point because the shunemite woman doesn't know that she has set the stage for a blessing in her life, well let's go on.

❖ She is a wise planner

This woman knew that if she hosted the man of God and kept him comfortable, her home will receive blessings. What kind of decisions do you make for your home? Are they to bless your home or to bless you? If you can allow me to sight an example right here; do you plan on how many outfits you will have and trips to the saloon or do you make plans that will benefit you and your generation to come like the shunemite woman did? As 21st century women we need to get a grip of what beauty is, it starts from the inside out not outside in! inner beauty never ages but the outside one does. How do you get inner beauty? From Christ your Designer, He has a plan for every one's life and in Jeremiah 29:11 says; For I know the plans I have for you," says the Lord. "They are plans for good and not for disaster, to give you a future and a hope.

He tells us the plan and thoughts He has towards us are of peace and to give us a future of hope. I can tell why this woman was a rich and influential woman because she was a wise planner not a spender! When you get a cheque or some money where is your first stop? Are you a giver or taker? Are you sowing for your coming generation or you just sow to yourself? These are good questions to ask yourself then you can audit your life and see where you are going wrong.

This lady was investing in the kingdom of God she was putting the Lord first in her life like in Matthew 6:33 that says; But seek ye first the kingdom of God, and his righteousness; and all these things shall be added unto you. Look at the reward she later gets; an heir to their property, the desire of her heart and shame was averted from her home. Can you imagine the shame, the mockers in her life felt? I challenge you career woman, are you that kind of woman? If not guess what! You can be one, our God is a good God, He always gives us second chances no matter the stage you are at, there is always room for change, hallelujah!

- ❖ She had good courage, faith in God and believed in Him.

These are very strong virtuous traits that this woman had and they helped her in difficult times. We all have hard times and bad things happening to us but how do we handle these issues that happen? We need faith and we need to harness our tongues to speak words of faith not of despair. Remember the scripture we talked about earlier in Proverbs 18:21 that says; Death and life are in the power of the tongue: and they that love it shall eat the fruit thereof. We have to be careful what we let out of our mouths especially as mothers when we are talking to our children and husbands. Your words create your world if you don't like the world you are living in then change your words. By world I don't mean the earth as a whole I am talking about your lifestyle and your surroundings. Start talking positive about the town or city you live in. pray for your neighborhood and your country do not criticize all the time and expect to have a good land you have to change what you speak over your land. I do now, but I wasn't like that before until I got a revelation from the Spirit of God that my tongue was poisoning my world not the devil, my tongue. And now I speak different I have stopped being a pessimist I am now an optimist, I pray for my country, my city, the weather, my child's school, my businesses, my workers, I mean everything I can think of I pray for it and talk positively about it even when the circumstances are looking negative. Then within no time I see the circumstances line up with the Word of God and things straighten out. So let us change the way we talk and start letting words that edify come out of our mouths.

The shunemite woman's child died and she did not panic! That is amazing isn't it? She didn't go hysterical and get out of control but was rather composed. I know all mothers need help from the Spirit of God on this one, I was so shocked when I read how composed she was wow! How could she be composed at such a time? The son she longed for was dead and she is saying it is well?! How can it be well when her son is dead? I will tell you; its because she knew God and believed in Him and she had working faith not dead faith, lip service kind of faith. She knew if that son was from God then no one will ever take him away from her because remember the word of God says the blessings of the Lord are without repentance, that means He doesn't take back gifts He gives us. Romans 11:29 says this; For God's gifts and his call can never be withdrawn. And in King James Version of the bible it says; For the gifts and calling of God are without repentance.

God never changes His mind once He gives you something, a gift from God is permanent, hallelujah! And so we see in 2Kings 4: 26-30 [run now, I pray thee, to meet her, and say unto her, Is it well with thee? is it well with thy husband? is it well with the child? And she answered, It is well. And when she came to the man of God to the hill, she caught him by the feet: but Gehazi came near to thrust her away. And the man of God said, Let her alone; for her soul is vexed within her: and the Lord hath hid it from me, and hath not told me.

Then she said, Did I desire a son of my lord? did I not say, Do not deceive me?

Then he said to Gehazi, Gird up thy loins, and take my staff in thine hand, and go thy way: if thou meet any man, salute him not; and if any salute thee, answer him not again: and lay my staff upon the face of the child. And the mother of the child said, As the Lord liveth, and as thy soul liveth, I will not leave thee. And he arose, and followed her.] that she was persistent and didn't give up on her miracle, she held on to the man of God until he went with her and gave her back her son. Girls we need to be persistent in our prayers and hold on to the

Word of God until it comes to pass, for the promises of God are yes and amen (which means so be it) in Christ Jesus.

Ok, let's do an audit of our lives, what happens in your home when there is a crisis maybe it's not a death but just a difficult situation could be there is no money? Who do you run to? Do you ever think of God or you run to a friend? Do you ever ask the Lord Holy Spirit for help and direction in such times or you go emotional? Remember that emotions move you to a certain direction mostly the flesh or carnal direction. What words do you speak in such times?

- ❖ She was a sower

Verse 23 gives us information that this woman would give to the prophet of the Lord very often even the husband mentions that it wasn't a new moon or Sabbath that means she gave not only once but she lived a lifestyle of giving. In Luke 6:38 which says;[give, and it shall be given unto you; good measure, pressed down, and shaken together, and running over, shall men give into your bosom. For with the same measure that ye mete withal it shall be measured to you again.] we know that to receive, you have to give and the shunemite woman knew that, in order to receive her blessings she would have to give. I don't know but, she seems to me to have been practicing the law of seed time and harvest. The Lord promised in His word Genesis 8:22 that this is a principle that will not end as long as the earth remains and our God is a faithful God who also never lies, hallelujah.

Numbers 23:19

God is not a man, that he should lie; neither the son of man, that he should repent: hath he said, and shall he not do it? or hath he spoken, and shall he not make it good?

Hebrews 6:18

That by two immutable things, in which it was impossible for God to lie, we might have a strong consolation, who have fled for refuge to lay hold upon the hope set before us:

Titus 1:2

In hope of eternal life, which God, that cannot lie, promised before the world began;

I will keep on insisting on this phrase that; now you know why this lady was rich and influential because she was a giver. Show me a giver and I will show you a wealthy person because that is the nature of God; our Lord God gave us His son so that we can have life and life more abundantly. Anyone who loves God has His nature in other words they also have a giving nature, I like to say that if you really love God then you will love to give, you know like begets like.

As the last word on this subject; maybe it's good to think about the scripture in the book of Galatians 6:7, where we are told that God is not mocked for whatsoever a man sows that shall he also reap.

- ❖ She was respectful

If you read the whole passage of 2 kings 4 you will realize that the shunemite woman did respect her husband a lot, she did nothing without consulting with her husband. Submission is not slavery its actually honor to a woman, submission proves that you have your power harnessed to be useful. Submission comes automatically if there is love shown by the husband to his wife. No woman can resist to submit to her own husband if she is loved by her husband. I know that is a word most women hate but it's actually honorable to submit to your own husband. You have heard the saying united we stand, divided we fall or let me get it closer home remember Matthew 18:18-20 that is the power of agreement, this is what it says; Verily I say unto you, Whatsoever ye shall bind on earth shall be bound in heaven: and whatsoever ye shall loose on earth shall be loosed in heaven. Again I say unto you, That if two of you shall agree on earth as touching any thing that they shall ask, it shall be done for them of my Father which is in heaven. For where two or three are gathered together in my name, there am I in the midst of them.

That is what most homes are missing and the enemy is taking advantage of the division in homes to break them and bring poverty and sickness. As a woman who is married you cannot stay without submission in your house otherwise you will be living in disobedience and the spirit of rebellion may be living in you, which of course cannot be from the Lord so a disobedient wife is partnering with the devil and that is why her home goes down the drain. Please remember I am talking about submission in the context of love, this is where the husband is doing his job to love the wife as Christ loves the Church. So in cases where there is love from the husband a wife is commanded by the Lord who created marriages to submit to her own husband. If there is a person who knows how to make a marriage work it's the Lord God Himself it was His idea to give Adam a helper. So if a wife follows what the Lord commands about her role in marriage then the honey moon never stops. Let's change that as 21st century women and be the women of God who will make their marriages work and have homes that are full of peace and love. We will talk more on this later but for now if you are a wife and your marriage is suffering, try submission.

You know there is something I realized that without respect to authority its very difficult to follow the Lord because the spirit of rebellion is present in lawless people, make sure you don't fall in that category of knowing it all; the bible tells us in the book of proverbs 15:5 that those who heed to correction are wise, so be a wise woman and see what God will do with your life and family.

HERE SHE COMES AGAIN

It is amazing that this shunemite woman comes up again in 2 Kings 8:1-6, this is what it says;

Then spake Elisha unto the woman, whose son he had restored to life, saying, Arise, and go thou and thine household, and sojourn wheresoever thou canst sojourn: for the Lord hath called for a famine; and it shall also come upon the land seven years. And the woman arose, and did after the saying of the man of God: and she went with her household, and sojourned in the land of the Philistines seven years.

And it came to pass at the seven years' end, that the woman returned out of the land of the Philistines: and she went forth to cry unto the king for her house and for her land. And the king talked with Gehazi the servant of the man of God, saying, Tell me, I pray thee, all the great things that Elisha hath done. And it came to pass, as he was telling the king how he had restored a dead body to life, that, behold, the woman, whose son he had restored to life, cried to the king for her house and for her land. And Gehazi said, My lord, O king, this is the woman, and this is her son, whom Elisha restored to life.

And when the king asked the woman, she told him. So the king appointed unto her a certain officer, saying, Restore all that was hers, and all the fruits of the field since the day that she left the land, even until now.

I believe there is no coincidence in the bible, if it is in there its there for a reason. The Lord must be trying to tell us something about this woman who was a partner of 'Elisha ministries' if you could allow me to use that phrase. The Lord is faithful to His people and warns them of calamities. The shunemite woman was preserved by the Lord her and her whole family, isn't it worth it to serve the Lord? This time if you noticed she took the prophecy from the man of God and it saved her family. This another benefit she reaped because of sowing into the kingdom of God, her family never went through the famine that lasted 7 years! That is not a short time is it? Of course not, I am sure there were neighbors around her or some of her friends whom she told what the word of the

Lord said through the prophet Elisha but as usual they ignored her. If you read the chapter before that, you will notice in this famine there were women who ate their own children, what a tragedy! But the Lord supplied all the needs of this faithful woman. Let me just insert this here and say have you realized how pessimistic people are when men/women of God who are true prophets of the Lord give a warning and people just ignore them? Or let me bring it closer home, when it's a time to sow into a certain Christian TV station like say TBN or GOD TV, Daystar or any other Christian channel in your area during their fund raising or missions week and several men and women of God are invited to speak the word of the Lord then, the woman or man of God quotes a figure that you think cannot be from God and mostly you hear people saying 'ah they just want my money God cannot give me what I want when I give that amount of money' have you ever heard of such people? And please do not misunderstand me, you cannot buy a miracle from God, never; it's just an act of obedience; or have you ever been one of them? Then learn from the shunemmite woman and obey the word of the Lord when given by women or men of God who are lead by the Holy Spirit believe me it works. God doesn't need anyone's money remember the earth and the fullness thereof belongs to Him.

Therefore a seed sown to the kingdom of God can protect you from future disasters, as happened in this case. So as modern women let us audit our lives again on this issue, does your family sow into the kingdom of God? This is an important question to ask yourself; as a mother or wife because the bible says in Matthew 6:19-21 that;

Lay not up for yourselves treasures upon earth, where moth and rust doth corrupt, and where thieves break through and steal: but lay up for yourselves treasures in heaven, where neither moth nor rust doth corrupt, and where thieves do not break through nor steal: for where your treasure is, there will your heart be also.

We are also told in, 1 Timothy 6:17-19 that;

Tell those who are rich in this world not to be proud and not to trust in their money, which will soon be gone. But their trust should be in the living God, who richly gives us all we need for our enjoyment. Tell them to use their money to do good. They should be rich in good works and should give generously to those in need, always being ready to share with others whatever God has given them. By doing this they will be storing up their treasure as a good foundation for the future so that they may take hold of real life.

So we are to store our treasures in a place where there is no thief or moth to destroy it and that is in heaven. It's actually an investment it helps us in the future, yes; giving to God's business is investing for your future. And when you need it you can withdraw from your account in heaven and bring it down here on earth to help you, but that is a different topic altogether. This is a tip we can borrow from the shunemmite woman because she was a wise investor, are you investing for your family? I will let you answer that.

And so this woman obeyed the man of God, Elisha and left to live in the land of the Philistines but when the seven years came to an end she came back to claim her land and possessions. And the Lord favored her with the King and she was restored for everything she owned plus the profit of the 7 years that she was gone! Now look at this, while she was gone as much as it was during a famine the Lord was multiplying her and so her latter was greater than her beginning. Do you remember Job in Job 42:10 and how the Lord restored to him double for all his trouble because of his obedience to the Lord even through adversity. Do you remember King David in I Samuel 30:18-19 when the Lord caused him to recover all after the raid in ziklag where he lost everything he owned. That is the kind of God we serve, he restores us and gives us double for all our trouble.

This passage also reminds me of John 2:5 remember, the first miracle that our Lord Jesus Christ did in the wedding at Cana of Galilee. Mary the mother of our Lord told the servants and I quote 'whatever he tells you do it'. This is what the shunemmite woman did she just did what the man of God told her. That is obedience and the bible tells us in 1Samuel 15:22 that obedience is better than sacrifice. This is actually the key to success in life if only we can obey in Deuteronomy 28:1-2 it says;

And it shall come to pass, if thou shalt hearken diligently unto the voice of the Lord thy God, to observe and to do all his commandments which I command thee this day, that the Lord thy God will set thee on high above all nations of the earth: 2 and all these blessings shall come on thee, and overtake thee, if thou shalt hearken unto the voice of the Lord thy God.

If you will hearken, which means to hear and do what the voice of the Lord tells us then you get the blessings. Many Christians have crammed verses in this chapter but don't walk in them. You know why? Because they only hear and don't do they are just hearers only and not doers. I know all 21st century women want success; here is how you get it, whatever the Lord tells you to do just do it, listen to the voice of the Lord God and do it; that is all you need to be a success in life. In fact this is what the Lord told Joshua to do if he needed success in all he did, lets read this together;

Joshua 1:8 (KJV)

This book of the law shall not depart out of thy mouth; but thou shalt meditate therein day and night, that thou mayest observe to do according to all that is written therein: for then thou shalt make thy way prosperous, and then thou shalt have good success.

Joshua 1:8 (NLT)

Study this Book of the Law continually. Meditate on it day and night so you may be sure to obey all that is written in it. Only then will you succeed.

Ok you will agree with me that we need to study a little more on this verse to know how can we succeed, the first thing we have to realize is that there is bad success if there is good success. So what is good success? Good success is what the Lord wants us to have and in Jeremiah 29:11 we know that the Lord's thoughts and plans towards us are for our good and to make us prosper. Ok with that in mind then we know that it's the Lord's will for us to have good success but how do we get it? We need to study Joshua 1:8 to know the answer to this question. Ok go with me through this study please if you will, as we keep on referring to the verse in the book of Joshua chapter 1, the 8th verse.

The first thing is to not let this book of the law (which is the Word of God that is the bible) not depart from your mouth.

So what does this mean? It means you should always be speaking the Word. Why? Because the Word of God says;

Proverbs 18:21

Death and life are in the power of the tongue: and they that love it shall eat the fruit thereof.

Proverbs 12:14

A man shall be satisfied with good by the fruit of his mouth: and the recompence of a man's hands shall be rendered unto him.

Proverbs 13:2

A man shall eat good by the fruit of his mouth: but the soul of the transgressors shall eat violence.

Proverbs 18:20

A man's belly shall be satisfied with the fruit of his mouth; and with the increase of his lips shall he be filled.

Matthew 12:34

O generation of vipers, how can ye, being evil, speak good things? for out of the abundance of the heart the mouth speaketh.

Luke 6:45

A good man out of the good treasure of his heart bringeth forth that which is good; and an evil man out of the evil treasure of his heart bringeth forth that which is evil: for of the abundance of the heart his mouth speaketh.

So from these scriptures we see that we live what we speak with our mouths so if we speak the Word of God then we will live the fullness that is in the Word of God which is as we have said good success. Another reason we see here is that people only speak what is in their hearts so whatever you fill your heart or mind with is what will come out of your mouth, do you see that? And that is why the Lord says we have to keep on saying what is in His Word and not stop, so that we fill our hearts with His Word and then it will come out of our mouths. Ok you may be asking why should we speak can't we just read it? No my friend we have to speak it you know why? There is power in speaking, in the verses we have just read above in proverbs it says life and death are in the power of the tongue, did you see that? And also remember we are created in the image of God (Genesis 1:26-27) and if you read the story of creation in this chapter of Genesis you will realize that God spoke this universe into existence. So think with me here, since we are made in the image and likeness of God then we can also speak creative words. That is why we are to speak the Word of God and what it says about us then we will have what we say. Words are creative the bible tells us we shall reap what we sow;

Galatians 6:7

Be not deceived; God is not mocked: for whatsoever a man soweth, that shall he also reap.

Galatians 6:8

For he that soweth to his flesh shall of the flesh reap corruption; but he that soweth to the Spirit shall of the Spirit reap life everlasting.

Words are seeds that can be sown and later bring in a harvest, oh yes have you ever heard someone say something over and over again and then later it happens? I have, in fact lots of times I have heard a mother call her child horrible names and then later when the child grows up they become exactly what the mother used to tell her. Do you know why that happens? Because the power of life and death are in the tongue. Pessimist always have miserable lives but if you get a person who is optimistic in her approach to life she seems to soar higher and higher in life stress free. The law of seed time and harvest is like the law of gravity just that it's also a spiritual law apart from a natural law of agriculture.

Ok now let us go on to the next step the second thing you have to do according to Joshua 1:8 is ; you are to meditate on this Word of God day and night. So what does day and night mean? You may ask, it means all the time not that you are not suppose to sleep and so read the Word 24 hours a day 7 days a week and 365 days a year; No, its just that you are to meditate on the Word of God all the time. All the time like when you are bathing in the morning, cooking, exercising, just before you go to bed, first thing in the morning when you awake from sleep, sometimes even in the middle of the night when you find yourself awake! Or doing whatever chores you can do while thinking. Which brings me to the next question which is what is to meditate? Meditate has several meanings we will look at a few of these which is to think about the Word of God, it could be maybe you read a scripture and you memorize it and keep on rolling it over and over in your mind and speaking to your inner self. Active listening to the Word like from CD, DVDs, tapes, radio, TV and all other listening devices out there, it could be it's a teaching series or just bible verses being read out. Sometimes you can even have music that is biblically based with a lot of lyrics from the scriptures and that can help you start thinking about the goodness of God and His works in your life and then you start praising Him. Studying the Word of God is also meditating. Reading the Word of God slowly and speaking it allowed to yourself is also meditating, it could also be in form of books addressing different topics in life that are full of scriptures that can help you meditate on the Word and build you up in that area of life, that is also another way you can meditate on the Word of God. I will close this subject of meditation with these scriptures in Psalms1:1-3;

Blessed is the man that walketh not in the counsel of the ungodly, nor standeth in the way of sinners, nor sitteth in the seat of the scornful.

But his delight is in the law of the Lord; and in his law doth he meditate day and night.

And he shall be like a tree planted by the rivers of water, that bringeth forth his fruit in his season; his leaf also shall not wither; and whatsoever he doeth shall prosper.

The third and last thing we are told to do in Joshua 1:8 is to do that is to act on what we read in the Word. In the book of James we are told that faith without works is dead. We are suppose to be doers of the Word not only hearers. Acting on the Word means that you obey what the Lord is saying. When the three are put together the Lord assures us that we will have good success, are you interested in having good success in all you do? Then make this scripture your lifestyle and it will come to pass. I pray this study has blessed you, you can apply it in all you do be it your single life or married life, raising up children or doing business, studying or working in your career and it you will always have good success in that area that you apply this scripture.

THE REAL WOMAN

There is a woman who outshines all these noble women; yes there is and this is the woman who reverently and worshipfully fears the Lord. She is the one who is called blessed by her children and her husband boasts about her and praises her all the time. This is no fairy tale its truth because the bible tells us in Proverbs 31 that it is possible for a woman to have all that.
Can you imagine that? Please do; imagine for a moment if you are a mother seeing your children coming right up to you and saying 'mummy you are so blessed, I love you and admire you, I am glad that you are my mother, God bless you mummy, I love you' that is my prayer for all who read this book and are mothers or mothers to be, may the Lord grant us this prayer as mothers, amen.

Please come along with me into this study of this ideal woman of God, she is the proverbs 31 woman and as we study her using other related scriptures in the word of God to understand how to be the real women that God created us to be.

We will start from Proverbs 31 and verse 10 all the way to 31 may the Lord Holy Spirit help you understand and I follow what the Lord is communicating to us through this proverb.

I would recommend that you read these verses in different versions of the bible so as to get better understanding on the whole subject if you would like to understand a little more on this, but for now here are the scriptures as they are in KJV;

Proverbs 31:10-31

Who can find a virtuous woman? for her price is far above rubies.

The heart of her husband doth safely trust in her, so that he shall have no need of spoil.

She will do him good and not evil all the days of her life.

She seeketh wool, and flax, and worketh willingly with her hands.

She is like the merchants' ships; she bringeth her food from afar.

She riseth also while it is yet night, and giveth meat to her household, and a portion to her maidens.

She considereth a field, and buyeth it: with the fruit of her hands she planteth a vineyard.

She girdeth her loins with strength, and strengtheneth her arms.

She perceiveth that her merchandise is good: her candle

goeth not out by night.

She layeth her hands to the spindle, and her hands hold the distaff.

She stretcheth out her hand to the poor; yea, she reacheth forth her hands to the needy.

She is not afraid of the snow for her household: for all her household are clothed with scarlet.

She maketh herself coverings of tapestry; her clothing is silk and purple.

Her husband is known in the gates, when he sitteth among the elders of the land.

She maketh fine linen, and selleth it; and delivereth girdles unto the merchant.

Strength and honour are her clothing; and she shall rejoice in time to come.

She openeth her mouth with wisdom; and in her tongue is the law of kindness.

She looketh well to the ways of her household, and eateth not the bread of idleness.

Her children arise up, and call her blessed; her husband also, and he praiseth her.

Many daughters have done virtuously, but thou excellest them all.

Favour is deceitful, and beauty is vain: but a woman that

feareth the Lord, she shall be praised.

Give her of the fruit of her hands; and let her own works praise her in the gates.

There are several characteristics that we note from this proverb that an ideal woman should have; verse 10 gives them to us. A woman should be capable to do her work, she is virtuous in other words it means lead by the Holy Spirit and lastly she is intelligent. So this then gives us an idea of how to bring up our young girls, they should be well trained in the field they excel in to make them capable of running with the task the Lord created them for, which goes hand in hand with intelligence so then the girl child should go to school to develop her intellectually. She should also grow spiritually in the things of God; this is by reading the bible and having an intimate relationship with Christ Jesus. The first step is to be born again.

THE GOLDEN OPPORTUNITY

So then at this point since we are learning who to be the real woman I would like to invite you if you have not yet accepted the son of God our Lord Jesus Christ as your savior and Lord you can do so right now by saying this short prayer in faith believing:

Say,

Father God in the name of Jesus I pray and I ask you to come into my heart. Lord Jesus forgive me of my sins and cleanse me with your blood. I believe that you are the son of God and you died on the cross for me and rose from the dead on the third day. I confess with my mouth right now that Jesus you are my Lord and savior. I renounce satan and all his works in my life. From now on I will live for you. I will be lead by the Holy Spirit all the days of my life. Thank you Lord for I am now a child of God, in Jesus name, Amen.

Congratulations if this was your first time to pray this prayer, now you are a child of the living God, (John1:12).

PRECIOUS VIRTUES

In proverbs 12:4 another character we observe there about this woman is an earnest and strong character which makes one a worthy wife and a crowning joy to her husband. The same is found in proverbs 31:25 where we are told that she puts on strength and dignity as her clothing making her position strong and secure.

In proverbs 18:22 we see that a good or true wife brings favor from the Lord. And as you see later in proverbs 31:23 the husband now is known in the city gates and is sitting with elders which means he is in a position of authority because of the favor the Lord has poured in the home.

She is prudent in her matters of business and house work. Along with that is understanding and in proverbs 19:14 says that this wife if from the Lord. If you read keenly you will realize she also has savings for her family. She is not a spender as some of the women are nowadays; spending hours in the malls and markets is good only if you have planned it but it should not be done by impulse. This is an area many modern women are not good at; remember as women of God we are in the world but not of the world (Romans 12:2).

Have you ever heard of wives complaining that their husbands don't trust them? I have. In fact many times I hear men saying that they cannot tell their wives of their investments or how much they have saved in their bank accounts because she will start giving a list of demands. Maybe this is only in Africa! But I think the primary reason of such statements is found in proverbs 31:11. Just maybe, I don't want to accuse women but just maybe, it could be that most wives are not confidential about their house matters. Since the word of God is absolutely true then we can take it and say that the reason some husbands hearts are not trusting to their wives is because the wives are not confidential. Because if they are then the husband will rely on and believe securely in his wife only!

There is another tip for wives in the next verse which gives them the role to encourage and comfort their husbands. The Lord also requires them to do only good towards them. A question comes to mind when I read this, what if what he is doing to his wife is not good? The bible says do good to him and let the Lord judge. Remember Abigail in 1Samuel 25,; Nabal her husband was a stupid man who did not do well to his wife in terms of protecting the family but she covered him by taking gifts to David to protect her family, you can read the rest to know what happened to Nabal.

Did you know that mothers yes, wives are supposed to be entrepreneurs? I have heard people say that a woman's position is in the kitchen that is all she is supposed to do, wrong! And neither is she to be an object of sex. The Lord tells us in proverbs 31:13 [She seeketh wool, and flax, and worketh willingly with her hands.] and verse 24 [She maketh fine linen, and selleth it; and delivereth girdles unto the merchant.]that this blessed woman of God is doing business on behalf of her family in fact it goes on to say she is a real estate manager for the home ah! Yes looks it up in verse 16 [She considereth a field, and buyeth it: with the fruit of her hands she planteth a vineyard.] farming is a business just as real estate is or whatever the Lord has laid in your heart as your family business.

And yet there are women in this 21st century whose names are not in legal ownership-documents like title deeds, log books and the like, its clear that this is not the will of God for such families.

Let us look at proverbs 31:17 [She girdeth her loins with strength, and strengtheneth her arms.] Here we see that she girds her loins with strength; do you know what this means? Its very important we know that loins is the waist but this is not talking about tying your waist with strength, no remember in the book of Ephesians 6 where it talks about the full armour of God here it is;

Ephesians 6: 10-18

Finally, my brethren, be strong in the Lord, and in the power of his might. Put on the whole armour of God, that ye may be able to stand against the wiles of the devil. For we wrestle not against flesh and blood, but against principalities, against powers, against the rulers of the darkness of this world, against spiritual wickedness in high places. Wherefore take unto you the whole armour of God, that ye may be able to withstand in the evil day, and having done all, to stand. Stand therefore, having your loins girt about with truth, and having on the breastplate of righteousness; and your feet shod with the preparation of the gospel of peace; above all, taking the shield of faith, wherewith ye shall be able to quench all the fiery darts of the wicked. And take the helmet of salvation, and the sword of the Spirit, which is the word of God: praying always with all prayer and supplication in the Spirit, and watching thereunto with all perseverance and supplication for all saints;

Notice in verse 17 we are told to put on the belt of truth which represents the Word of God according to the book of John so it cannot be the natural waist the Lord is talking about here its actually the mind. So we gird our mind with the truth which is the Word of God. But in Proverbs 31:17 as we have seen also talks about girding our mind with strength, now here is what I am leading you to; remember the Lord is our strength we can see this in several scriptures lets look at some of them;

Exodus 15:2

The Lord is my strength and my song; he has become my victory. He is my God, and I will praise him; he is my father's God, and I will exalt him!

Psalms 18:1

I will love thee, O LORD, my strength.

Psalms 18:2

The LORD is my rock, and my fortress, and my deliverer; my God, my strength, in whom I will trust; my buckler, and the horn of my salvation, and my high tower.

Psalms 19:14

Let the words of my mouth, and the meditation of my heart, be acceptable in thy sight, O LORD, my strength, and my redeemer.

Isaiah 26:4

Trust ye in the LORD for ever: for in the LORD JEHOVAH is everlasting strength:

So an ideal woman will put on the Lord as her strength by reading His Word that is the only way to protect and gird up your mind with the Lord Himself who is the Word of God (John 1:1 and 14). So as ideal women of God then reading the

Word of God daily and all the time as we talked earlier on meditation will give us strength and therefore keep us away from an idle mind which then leads to gossiping instead of building others.

She also has strong hands those comes from toning your muscles with exercise. Women need to exercise oh yes I didn't like it either but its keeping the temple of the Lord which is our body, fit and healthy so that we can have energy to serve our Lord and Redeemer. Being a hard working woman will lead to having strong hands slothful hands cannot have any muscle in them. The real woman is supposed to be strong all round by this I mean physically, spiritually and mentally. Remember 3rd John 2 we are suppose to prosper spirit, soul and body. Mentally we are to renew our minds with the word of God that is food for the soul which comprises of our emotions, will and thoughts. The word of God says we are what we think;

Proverbs 23:7

For as he thinketh in his heart, so is he: Eat and drink, saith he to thee; but his heart is not with thee.

And we have several gateways to the soul, like we have the eyes and ears so you have to watch and read what is edifying to your soul otherwise garbage in is garbage out. And then for our ears what we listen to like the songs or the talk we engage in or what we let other people say to us matters, the apostle Paul told us we should think about good and lovely things.

Philippians 4:8.

Finally, brethren, whatsoever things are true, whatsoever things are honest, whatsoever things are just, whatsoever things are pure, whatsoever things are lovely, whatsoever things are of good report; if there be any virtue, and if there be any praise, think on these things.

Then we have the spiritual element, and this is where we are born again and led by the Spirit of God, having quality time with the Lord in prayer not 5 seconds before you fall asleep! Studying and reading the Word of God every day, you know you can read the Word of God from several sources it could be the bible or books that are full of the scriptures, sometimes you can have articles written by men and women of God that can help you meditate on the Word. Praying in the spirit, this means leaving the Holy Spirit lead you in your prayers as it is written in Romans 8:26-27

Likewise the Spirit also helpeth our infirmities: for we know not what we should pray for as we ought: but the Spirit itself maketh intercession for us with groanings which cannot be uttered. And he that searcheth the hearts knoweth what is the mind of the Spirit, because he maketh intercession for the saints according to the will of God.

Physical fitness is something most people do not concentrate on and yet our body is the temple of the Lord.

1 Corinthians 6:19

Or don't you know that your body is the temple of the Holy Spirit, who lives in you and was given to you by God? You do not belong to yourself,

So we need to keep it fit by brisk walking, running, lifting weights, aerobics, swimming, riding the bike, skipping rope and many other fun things that get your metabolism moving. Of course this is coupled with eating healthy meals not junk food. Try and eat food as close to what the Lord created. Avoid if you can over processed foods. As women we can save lives in this world by teaching our children and family members how to eat healthy home made food. I know sometimes if a wife or mother is working it can get hectic to prepare fresh cooked food but also I believe with the technology of freezers and microwaves we can make healthy home made food for our families. The dishes will not be a problem if you think of the health benefits and anyway there are dish washers. Food can be made attractive to eat by doing simple little things like using spices or buy marinated meats to spare yourself the time to marinate, use different kind of sauces to spice up the meals, these are just little tips and I am sure you have many more that can help our families look healthy. Supplementing with vitamins if one can afford it and a wise woman does this for her whole family, do not let your children or husband lag behind let health fitness be a family thing. This ideal woman is not lazy at all.

Just like the shunemite woman in verse 20 we find that this woman is a giver. She gives to the poor and needy. If you would like your family as a wife to prosper financially please consider this, it's vital. The word of the Lord tells us in Luke 6:38 to give, other scriptures that you can meditate and study are Mark 10:29-30 and Proverbs 19:17. Any wise woman who loves her family will listen to the Lord on this issue and do it. I could tell you of a testimony one after another in my own life and others but it's your time to get your own testimony because the word of God works for everyone who is willing hallelujah!

Another very vital thing this woman does is she gets the Lords covering over her family. Proverbs 31:21, her whole family is clothes with scarlet. Scarlet is red so why red? I think it represents the covering of sin by blood and as we all know the blood that washes all the sins away and makes us white as snow is the blood of Jesus Christ. Just for you to study you can read Leviticus 14:14 and also in Exodus 12 just to appreciate the role of the Blood of the Passover Lamb, which in the new covenant is the Blood of Christ Jesus the Passover Lamb of God. We should cover our family members and possessions daily with the blood of Christ to keep away the enemy. I think a wise woman should do that for her family it's vital, I do that myself. Here are some of the scriptures that can help you understand this issue of the blood of Jesus Christ and how important it is to us;

Hebrews 9:11-26

But Christ being come an high priest of good things to come, by a greater and more perfect tabernacle, not made with hands, that is to say, not of this building; neither by the blood of goats and calves, but by his own blood he entered in once into the holy place, having obtained eternal redemption for us.

For if the blood of bulls and of goats, and the ashes of an heifer sprinkling the unclean, sanctifieth to the purifying of the flesh: how much more shall the blood of Christ, who through the eternal Spirit offered himself without spot to God, purge your conscience from dead works to serve the living God? And for this cause he is the mediator of the new testament, that by means of death, for the redemption of the transgressions that were under the first testament, they which are called might receive the promise of eternal inheritance. For where a testament is, there must also of necessity be the death of the testator. For a testament is of force after men are dead: otherwise it is of no strength at all while the testator liveth. Whereupon neither the first testament was dedicated without blood. For when Moses had spoken every precept to all the people according to the law, he took the blood of calves and of goats, with water, and scarlet wool, and hyssop, and sprinkled both the book, and all the people, saying, This is the blood of the testament which God hath enjoined unto you. Moreover he sprinkled with blood both the tabernacle, and all the vessels of the ministry. And almost all things are by the law purged with blood; and without shedding of blood is no remission.

It was therefore necessary that the patterns of things in the heavens should be purified with these; but the heavenly things themselves with better sacrifices than these.

For Christ is not entered into the holy places made with hands, which are the figures of the true; but into heaven itself, now to appear in the presence of God for us: nor yet that he should offer himself often, as the high priest entereth into the holy place every year with blood of others; for then must he often have suffered since the foundation of the world: but now once in the end of the world hath he appeared to put away sin by the sacrifice of himself.

Ephesians 1:7

In whom we have redemption through his blood, the forgiveness of sins, according to the riches of his grace;

Hebrews 10:4

For it is not possible that the blood of bulls and of goats should take away sins.

1 John 1:7

But if we walk in the light, as he is in the light, we have fellowship one with another, and the blood of Jesus Christ his Son cleanseth us from all sin.

In verse 22 of proverbs 31 you will realize that is talking about a fine linen garment that the ideal woman clothes herself with. Could you please turn with me to the book of Isaiah 61:10 [I will greatly rejoice in the Lord, my soul shall be joyful in my God; for he hath clothed me with the garments of salvation, he hath covered me with the robe of righteousness, as a bridegroom decketh himself with ornaments, and as a bride adorneth herself with her jewels.]you will realize that the garment that the Lord was clothing them with is the garment of salvation and a covering of righteousness. Now in 2Corinthians 5:21[For he hath made him to be sin for us, who knew no sin; that we might be made the righteousness of God in him.] the word says that we are the righteousness of God in Christ. This also can be seen in Revelation 19:8 [And to her was granted that she should be arrayed in fine linen, clean and white: for the fine linen is the righteousness of saints.] where fine linen represents godly living and righteousness. Our righteousness is Christ so as ideal women we should cloth ourselves with Christ as our covering, hallelujah!

She is a woman also who follows the advice that Apostle Paul gives in Titus 2:3-5 [3 The aged women likewise, that they be in behaviour as becometh holiness, not false accusers, not given to much wine, teachers of good things; that they may teach the young women to be sober, to love their husbands, to love their children, to be discreet, chaste, keepers at home, good, obedient to their own husbands, that the word of God be not blasphemed.] older women are to give good instruction to the younger ones and pass on godly wisdom to them, while at the same time telling the young wives what to engage in: As we have sow earlier not in gossip but in hard work. I don't know about you but, I have seen women especially in suburbs where they sit in groups and all they do is gossip. Then I have seen others who are in middle class dwellings and they are house wives and all they do with their friends when they meet is to talk of how sorry they feel for themselves which is self pity . And if that is not the case the very rich ones always complain of how they are not doing so well like so and so that means they are discontent. I love the bible because it never leaves anyone out, it's all inclusive. Now with that in mind let's read proverbs 31:27. It is talking about the bread of idleness which is what I have just been sighting above. Do you now see why many families never improve? its because of reaping what they have been sowing with their mouth, so if you want to see different results in your home start sowing different kinds of seed. We talked earlier about the power of life and death is found in the tongue, so this is the same concept.

THE ULTIMATE RESULT

I don't know about men but at least since I am a woman I can say this; the thing that every woman longs for in life is to be appreciated and loved, do you agree with me ladies?. If you would please, let us read together proverbs 31:28 [Her children arise up, and call her blessed; her husband also, and he praiseth her.] wow! Isn't that something that every woman, wife or mother would want? To be called blessed by your children and for your husband to be praising you all the time and boasting about you being his wife, hey it's possible! Don't say it's not possible, in fact it can happen to you oh yes to you! But how you ask? Simple, just learn how to reverently and worshipfully fear the Lord, yes that is the answer the Lord gives us in verse 30 part b of this wonderful proverb. [Favour is deceitful, and beauty is vain: but a woman that feareth the Lord, she shall be praised.]And so this is the **KEY** to being the ideal woman.

I know you must be asking but how can I reverently and worshipfully fear the Lord, Liz? Well let's take another trip and the Lord Holy Spirit will show us how to be the real women God created us to be. Are you ready for another study trip? Ok here we go!

TO REVERENTLY AND WORSHIPFULLY FEAR THE LORD

The word of God is the absolute truth in this matter and the only manual we have to help us know how to be ideal women of God. And so I have selected with the help of my Lord Holy Spirit some of these verses for you to read and see how you can learn how to fear the Lord. The fear we are talking about here is not the fear that brings torment to us but it's a word used to refer to the respect you have for God and the awe and reverence we give to Him. The word of the Lord says perfect love removes all fear because fear brings torment. And fear anyway comes from the devil so this is not what I am talking about here where you see God as some strict ready to punish person not at all, God is love and He loves us so much that He died for us on the cross that is perfect love that removes all fear. So with that clear then we can now go on and see that scripture that can help us learn how to reverently fear and worship the Lord.

1 John 4:18

There is no fear in love; but perfect love casteth out fear: because fear hath torment. He that feareth is not made perfect in love.

Leviticus 25:17

Ye shall not therefore oppress one another; but thou shalt fear thy God: for I am the LORD your God.

Here we see that we show the fear of the Lord by not oppressing others. What does the word oppress mean? I realized it means a whole lot than just what one may think by just reading this verse, let me share with you some of the meanings of this word and you will realize how vital this is. Oppress means; to subjugate, to repress, to keep someone down, to tyrannize, to dominate someone, to coerce. These are but a few of the synonyms of this word oppress and if you look around and judge yourself you will realize many people nowadays do repress others especially in third world countries where many women are working and have house helps (people who help them do house chores) or nanny for their children and for example if a woman doesn't pay them well enough or she lets them work long hours without rest or verbally insult them and many things that happen in homes. Any woman doing this does not fear the Lord, that is what this verse is telling us as women. I will not go into detail on this I think you can do a good job yourself by judging what you do to those who help you around your home. By the way this is not necessarily for domestic workers we could also have people working for you in your office or business how do you care for your workers? That is basically what the Lord is trying to get us as women to think about. The Lord told us to love one another for that is the witness that we are of Him.

Deuteronomy 4:10

Specially the day that thou stoodest before the LORD thy God in Horeb, when the LORD said unto me, Gather me the people together, and I will make them hear my words, that they may learn to fear me all the days that they shall live upon the earth, and that they may teach their children.

Hearing the Word of God and doing it shows the fear of the

Lord. Disobedience is a sign of lack of the fear of God in ones life. That is why its important for us to not only go to church but also read the Word and do what it says we should do. We should not only be women who when they hear the Word jump and yell and then once out of the church or meeting forget all about the Word and not do it. We should be doers of the Word so that we see results from practicing and living the Word.

I have seen this work in my life where before I became intimate with the Word of the Lord I would just read it as a story book and try and memorize some verses that I thought were nice and a day after that I would have forgotten all that as if I hadn't read it at all. I even had a schedule of reading the whole bible once every year but I had no Word in me at all. I know that sounds surprising but it's true. I had to learn to invite the Spirit of God to teach me and make me understand the bible then I started getting rhema words out of the written word. I thought I should share this with you just to encourage you to read the Word of God and not just reading it lightly. The Word of God started working for me in my life when I started studying the Word and meditating on it. Its after reading the Word of God like that, that I got free from depression and anger that was robbing me of abundant life. If it worked for me it will work for you, so please its never too late to start on the right path; if you missed the mark the way I did, start all over again and see how the Word works for you. Remember God is no respecter of persons what he does for one He will do for another.

Deuteronomy 6:2

That thou mightest fear the LORD thy God, to keep all his statutes and his commandments, which I command thee, thou, and thy son, and thy son's son, all the days of thy life; and that thy days may be prolonged.

This is one benefit of having the fear of the Lord, that is to have long life, we see from this scripture that we get long life not only for ourselves but for our children and grandchildren what a heritage! We as mothers can give our lineage a history of long life, would you like that? Its just by obeying the word of God and keeping His commandments. I would love to give this benefit to my son and grandchildren wouldn't you? There is a word here I would like us to understand its meaning because I found it very interesting during my study and it's the word; Keep. Keep means to hear, receive, love and obey; isn't that interesting that the Lord would tell us in order to show Him reverential fear we need to keep all His statutes or commandments if you will. That means we are to love them, hear them, receive them and obey them, wow! What a word to meditate on. Just take a few moments and think about the meaning of this word, then reflect it to your own life and see if you are one of those reverently fearing the Lord because as you have read the benefit is great to both us and our children and grandchildren.

Deuteronomy 14:23

And thou shalt eat before the LORD thy God, in the place which he shall choose to place his name there, the tithe of thy corn, of thy wine, and of thine oil, and the firstlings of thy herds and of thy flocks; that thou mayest learn to fear the LORD thy God always.

Giving tithes and first fruits show the fear of the Lord in our lives.

Oh, yes I know this is a touchy issue but it's the truth and the Truth sets us free. It did set me free when my finances were a mess. The only thing here is as we said earlier its your obedient heart, this is not a commandment that you have to do or a matter of salvation of your soul, no it's a matter of obedience and desire to live an abundant life. I hate poverty its ugly, I just do not like it and that is why I chose to obey the Lord on this issue because I was tired of lack. So just to help you if you are interested to know the difference between a tithe and first fruit. A tithe is the tenth that is 10 out of 100 of your income while the first fruit is the first of the whole for example if you are a farmer and have 100 bulls that you sell to get beef then the first bull you sell is your first fruit while the tithe of the sale of these bulls would the 10% of the income you got after the sale. I hope I have made it clear for you. And if you want if you want to study more on this issue of tithe and first fruit then you read the following scriptures: Malachi 3, Nehemiah 10, Deuteronomy chapters 12,14 and 26, Ezekiel 44:30, Proverbs 3:9. These are just a few to help you started on your study on this, God bless you.

Psalms 112:1

Praise ye the LORD. Blessed is the man that feareth the LORD, that delighteth greatly in his commandments.

What does it mean to delight in His commandments? I asked myself this questions severally when I would read this word in the bible because I wanted the Lord to give me the desires of my heart and in Psalms 37:4 it says you have to delight yourself in the Lord then He will give you the desires of your heart, so anyway this is what it means; it means to enjoy or to take pleasure in that means then if you enjoy the commandments of the Lord if they are a joy for you to hear them and do an dif you take pleasure in them then you are reverently fearing the Lord.

Psalms 128:1

Blessed is every one that feareth the LORD; that walketh in his ways

Walking in the ways of the Lord means to follow or obey His Word.

Psalms 147:11

The LORD taketh pleasure in them that fear him, in those that hope in his mercy.

Proverbs 8:13

The fear of the LORD is to hate evil: pride, and arrogancy, and the evil way, and the froward mouth, do I hate.

Proverbs 14:2

He that walketh in his uprightness feareth the LORD: but he that is perverse in his ways despiseth him.

Proverbs 15:33

The fear of the LORD is the instruction of wisdom; and before honour is humility.

Isaiah 11:2

And the spirit of the LORD shall rest upon him, the spirit of wisdom and understanding, the spirit of counsel and might, the spirit of knowledge and of the fear of the LORD;

The Spirit of God is the one who gives us the spirit of the fear of the Lord, this is a blessing to me because its amazing how much we get from the Holy Spirit there is nothing I can do without Him. If you find it difficult to fear the Lord just ask the Lord Holy Spirit and He will give you the spirit of the fear of the Lord.

Malachi 3:16

Then they that feared the LORD spake often one to another: and the LORD hearkened, and heard it, and a book of remembrance was written before him for them that feared the LORD, and that thought upon his name.

People who fear the Lord talk about Him with one another and think about the name of the Lord, so it means they love the Lord so much that they keep on talking about His goodness towards them, so a question for you here is; what do you talk about when you are with your friends women talk a lot but what we talk about is what matters.

Talking about the Lord will bring the book of remembrance out. Whenever I read this I always remember the story in the book of Esther about her uncle Mordecai where king Xerxes could not sleep and then he was read for the book of remembrance which was a book that keeps a record of all the people who did a good deed to the king and their rewards and so Mordecai was rewarded by the king on the day he was to be hanged and guess who was given the honor of making sure all the rewards were perfect? Yes it was his enemy who wanted to kill him on that same day. No wonder the bible says no weapon formed against us (we who love the Lord) shall ever prosper; you can read this in Esther 2:21-23 and chapter 6. The other thing we see sighted here is those who reverently fear the Lord think about Him. You will agree with me that you can only think of someone you love or someone you spend a lot of time with, right? There is a wonderful summary I like that the bible gives concerning the fear of the Lord, it is found in the 8th chapter of Proverbs and verse 13 this is what it says:

The fear of the Lord is to hate evil: pride, and arrogance, and the evil way, and the froward mouth, do I hate.

The amplified version of the bible puts it like this:

The reverent fear and worshipful awe of the Lord [includes] the hatred of evil, pride ,arrogance, the evil way and perverted and twisted speech I hate.

What a straight forward way to put it, you want to be an ideal woman of God then do these things the Lord has talked about here;

- ❖ Hate evil- what is evil? Evil is immorality, wickedness, iniquity, sin these are just but few words to try and explain what evil is. And so if you hate these things then it means you do not do them. In Christ our sins are forgiven and all our iniquities. In Christ we are pure and righteous.

- ❖ Hate pride – pride and arrogance go together it's a way of feeling self important, a person who is egotistic could also be in this category. Someone who feels superior to others in one way or another. The bible tells us that pride comes before a fall and the Lord hates it. These are some scriptures from the New Living Translation of the bible that tells us more on pride;

Proverbs 16:5

The Lord despises pride; be assured that the proud will be punished.

1 Timothy 3:6

An elder must not be a new Christian, because he might be proud of being chosen so soon, and the Devil will use that pride to make him fall.

- ❖ Hate arrogance
- ❖ Hate the evil way
- ❖ Hate perverted and twisted speech

You will notice that this phrase of the fear of the Lord is used often in the old covenant and just a few times in the new covenant. We see here the Apostle Paul telling us by the leading of the Holy Spirit that, we perfect holiness in the fear of the Lord our God.

2 Corinthians 7:1

Having therefore these promises, dearly beloved, let us

cleanse ourselves from all filthiness of the flesh and spirit, perfecting holiness in the fear of God.

There is another element of the fear of the Lord is; it is wisdom.

THE WISDOM OF GOD

Wisdom is the knowledge or the ability to make right choices and so you can only make right choices in life if you have the fear of the Lord in you. That is why the Word says the fear of the Lord is the beginning having the ability to make right choices.

Proverbs 9:10
Fear of the Lord is the beginning of wisdom. Knowledge of the Holy One results in understanding.
Psalms 111:10
The fear of the Lord is the beginning of wisdom: a good understanding have all they that do his commandments: his praise endureth for ever.

In both verses it says that the fear of the Lord is the beginning of wisdom and did you know that Wisdom is a person? Go with me if you will please to the book of 1 Corinthians 1:24 and verse 30 it says;

But unto them which are called, both Jews and Greeks, Christ the power of God, and the wisdom of God.

But of him are ye in Christ Jesus, who of God is made unto us wisdom, and righteousness, and sanctification, and redemption:

As you can see from these two verses; our Lord Jesus Christ is the wonderful wisdom of God. Do you have Wisdom? Yes, you do if you made Christ Jesus your Lord and Savior if not then, you do not have the wisdom of God. Those who are not born again do have wisdom but not from God. There are different kinds of wisdom; earthly, sensual and devilish wisdom, which also produces fruit and its fruit is strife, confusion, evil works and envy.

James 3:13-16

Who is a wise man and endued with knowledge among you? let him shew out of a good conversation his works with meekness of wisdom. But if ye have bitter envying and strife in your hearts, glory not, and lie not against the truth. This wisdom descendeth not from above, but is earthly, sensual, devilish. For where envying and strife is, there is confusion and every evil work.

But the wisdom from God is Jesus Christ and there are fruits of the wisdom of God that are the same as the fruits of the Holy Spirit. There is a scripture comparison I would like us to make and see how amazing it is that the Fruits of the Holy Spirit are the same as the Fruits of Wisdom. You know that the Holy Trinity is One God in three Persons that is Father, Son and Holy Spirit but they are One. So have a look with me at these verses in the book Galatians and James.

Galatians 5:22-23

But the fruit of the Spirit is love, joy, peace, longsuffering, gentleness, goodness, faith, meekness, temperance: against such there is no law.

James 3:17

But the wisdom that is from above is first pure, then peaceable, gentle, and easy to be intreated, full of mercy and good fruits, without partiality, and without hypocrisy.

This is wonderful to know, so if you have Christ Jesus in your heart as your personal Savior and filled with the Spirit of God you will have the fruits of wisdom flowing out of you. As we said earlier having the Lord Jesus Christ in the inside of you that is living in your heart is having Wisdom right? And now we see that those who are filled with the Spirit of Christ since they have Wisdom living in them no wonder the produce the same fruits of the Spirit. I hope this is clear to you now. In the earlier chapters we had talked about how one can be born again and filled with the Holy Spirit so that they can walk in and be lead by the Spirit of God. So if you add this information to that then you will see that there is no reason not to understand the Holy Trinity its that simple our God is One and He has three Persons in Him, so its not three gods; its One God in three Persons. The three Persons of God have different roles just the same way as I had explained earlier that you as a person has three different parts of you the spirit, soul and body. So that spirit has a different role, the soul's role is different that is where you think, have emotions and will and then all this is housed in your body, you see that? Our God is not the author of confusion He is order and that is why I am spending some time on this issue because it was also very confusing to me when I first came to Christ. But I thank God for His Holy Spirit that taught me very clearly the truth of the Holy Trinity as I have shared with you. So I hope this explanation will be of help to you if you had a hard time understanding this subject as I once did.

So far we have learnt that to be an ideal woman you need to reverence the Lord and worshipfully fear Him. If you do that, then you are at the beginning of wisdom. Christ Jesus is the wisdom of God as we have established from the verses we read above. You can use these verses to audit your life and see if the Wisdom of God and the Spirit of God are operating in your life by looking at the fruits that you have and compare them to those that are of God. If you find that you are lacking most or all of them there is nothing to be sorry about just repent and start all over again the bible tells us that if we do not have Wisdom we can ask the Lord and He will give us[James 1:5-8 says; If any of you lack wisdom, let him ask of God, that giveth to all men liberally, and upbraideth not; and it shall be given him. But let him ask in faith, nothing wavering. For he that wavereth is like a wave of the sea driven with the wind and tossed. For let not that man think that he shall receive any thing of the Lord. A double minded man is unstable in all his ways.] Why don't you do that right now, if you do not have the fruits of the wisdom of God in your life. Yes just stop right here and pray that the Lord will give you Wisdom He said that He will give you if you ask Him, do it right now and start enjoying the fruits of the wisdom of God.

I would like us to go deeper into this subject and study the verses in the book of Proverbs because only by reading and studying the word of God will we get a revelation of this truth and then it will help us be the ideal women God wants us to be. I know it's going to be a long study but we will use selected verses and then in your own free time you can read the 4 chapters on your own, you will realize that it is Christ that king Solomon was talking about. In this study we will also realize that there is a spirit of wisdom that the Lord talks about and it is the Lord Holy Spirit. Another interesting thing we will learn in these chapters is that the Lord refers to wisdom as a female, this really amazed me but what an honor it is to we as women that the Lord would even consider to refer to His wisdom as a female; this just blesses my heart and I hope it does yours. This aspect of Wisdom being referred as 'she', should not bring any confusion in your mind because we are not talking about female in a physical sense but in a spiritual sense so that this in mind as you read on. I do not know why the Lord chose to use this pronoun for His wisdom but we know that God in all His Wisdom was communicating something which we need to find out what it is, He is all knowing and Sovereign, please my friend keep this in mind as we do this study together. So let's dive in the waters of the word of God and learn more about this.

PROVERBS (SELECTED VERSES)

Proverbs 1:20 and 23

Wisdom crieth without; she uttereth her voice in the streets:

Turn you at my reproof: behold, I will pour out my spirit unto you, I will make known my words unto you.

Verse 23 in the Amplified version says this; *if you will turn (repent) and give heed to my reproof, behold I [Wisdom] will pour out my spirit upon you, I will make my words known to you.*

Verse 33 in the same version says; **But whoso hearkens to me [Wisdom] shall dwell securely and in confident trust and shall be quiet without fear or dread of evil.**

You will realize here that the wisdom of God who we now know is, Christ Jesus, is referred to with a female pronoun; 'she', in my curiosity I always wondered why? I asked the Lord Holy Spirit about this and He enlightened me; It is not about the gender as such and as I said earlier its not the physical aspect that we are looking at but rather the spiritual, the role is what is most important. So think with me here if you will please, what is the woman's role in creation? Her role is to bring forth life that was her role from creation, isn't it? Yes, we are on the right truck and the wisdom of God is Christ Jesus who was in the beginning during creation and without Him was nothing made that was made. So follow me closely here and now lets go to the book of John chapter 1 and verse 4 but lets back up and start in verse 3 and this is what it says;

John 1:1-3

In the beginning was the Word, and the Word was with God, and the Word was God. The same was in the beginning with God. All things were made by him; and

without him was not any thing made that was made. In him was life; and the life was the light of men.

He is life and if He is life does then He is the life giver because that is what we are trying to establish here, women bring forth life so does Christ bring forth life? Remember the bible says we have to be born again not by going back to our mothers' womb but spiritually by accepting the Son of God Jesus Christ into our hearts to be our Lord and Savior. So Christ gives us eternal life while women give natural life. Look at these verses;

John 11:25

Jesus said unto her, I am the resurrection, and the life: he that believeth in me, though he were dead, yet shall he live:

John 14:6

Jesus saith unto him, I am the way, the truth, and the life: no man cometh unto the Father, but by me.

John 8:12

Then spake Jesus again unto them, saying, I am the light of the world: he that followeth me shall not walk in darkness, but shall have the light of life.

1 John 5:20

And we know that the Son of God is come, and hath given us an understanding, that we may know him that is true, and we are in him that is true, even in his Son Jesus Christ. This is the true God, and eternal life.

So I hope with these verses you have seen for yourself that Christ Jesus is the giver of life and so Him being the wisdom of God he brings forth life. What a privilege He gave us as women to bring forth human life as He did eternal life. So if you are as curious as I am I hope you have the answer to your question, this right here gives me a special feeling and knowing that God gave me as a woman the responsibility to bring forth human life just as He brings forth eternal life wow!

After dealing with curiosity let's find out more on the wisdom of God, please keep in mind that we need the wisdom of God to learn how to fear and reverence the Lord which leads us to becoming ideal women of God. Ok then let's look at the reason why verse 20 says that the wisdom of God is crying aloud in the market places, read with me verse 23

Proverbs 1:23

Turn you at my reproof: behold, I will pour out my spirit unto you, I will make known my words unto you.

In the amplified version it refers to turning as repent, so the wisdom of God is telling us to repent then the Lord will pour out His spirit on us. Talking about the Spirit of the Lord reminds me of Isaiah 11:2 that says;

And the spirit of the Lord shall rest upon him, the spirit of wisdom and understanding, the spirit of counsel and might, the spirit of knowledge and of the fear of the Lord;

We are introduced to the spirit of wisdom this is the seven fold Spirit of God our Lord Holy Spirit. Would you please think with me on this verse a while; you cannot separate a person from their spirit right? For example my name is Liz so the spirit of Liz is Liz isn't that true? If you separate Liz the body from her spirit she will be dead right? So Liz and the spirit of Liz are one person because the spirit of Liz speaks through the body we are calling Liz, but in essence the real Liz is the spirit Liz.

Ephesians 1:17

That the God of our Lord Jesus Christ, the Father of glory, may give unto you the spirit of wisdom and revelation in the knowledge of him:

Well hope I got you thinking, following this argument then the Spirit of the Lord is the Lord Himself that means the Spirit of Wisdom is Wisdom. The Father, Son and Holy Spirit are ONE, hallelujah!

To make it easy on our study let us read the whole passage from verse 20 to 33 of chapter 1 from the book of proverbs;

Wisdom crieth without; she uttereth her voice in the streets:

She crieth in the chief place of concourse, in the openings of the gates: in the city she uttereth her words, saying,

How long, ye simple ones, will ye love simplicity? and the scorners delight in their scorning, and fools hate knowledge?

Turn you at my reproof: behold, I will pour out my spirit unto you, I will make known my words unto you.

Because I have called, and ye refused; I have stretched out my hand, and no man regarded;

But ye have set at nought all my counsel, and would none of my reproof:

I also will laugh at your calamity; I will mock when your fear cometh;

When your fear cometh as desolation, and your destruction cometh as a whirlwind; when distress and anguish cometh upon you.

Then shall they call upon me, but I will not answer; they shall seek me early, but they shall not find me:

For that they hated knowledge, and did not choose the fear of the Lord:

They would none of my counsel: they despised all my reproof.

Therefore shall they eat of the fruit of their own way, and be filled with their own devices.

For the turning away of the simple shall slay them, and the prosperity of fools shall destroy them.

But whoso hearkeneth unto me shall dwell safely, and shall be quiet from fear of evil.

There are consequences to listening or not listening to the voice of the wisdom of God, they could be positive or negative depending on what you choose. I am sure you are reading this book because you want to choose the positive results which are in the last verse. In amplified version of the bible the benefits of obedience to the voice of wisdom come out very clearly and if you may allow me to state it:

Verse 33: But whoso hearkens to me [Wisdom] shall dwell securely and in confident trust and shall be quiet without fear or dread of evil. There they are; security, confidence and trust in the Lord, quietness and no fear. Wow these are quite some promises from God that we all as women need in our homes, places of work, when our children are in school and community as a whole. I hope you notice that none of these can be bought; they only come from the Wisdom of God our Lord Jesus Christ.

The Wisdom of God is to be sought, I mean you have to seek for the Wisdom of God in order to find it, right here and now we are seeking it so that we can find it and get the treasures it has for us. Let me draw your attention to this word 'seek' it interests me a lot because I have found that precious things do not come easy, you have to look and search for them. I don't know if this has been your experience but it has been for me and so let us look at what the bible talks about seeking. Seeking in simple English means to search for or look for, so if you keep this meaning at the back of your mind it will amaze you what you will find out in the following verses that I pray will bless your heart and give you a hunger to keep on searching for the Lord with all your heart and mind and strength, have a look at these:

Deuteronomy 4:29

But if from thence thou shalt seek the LORD thy God, thou shalt find him, if thou seek him with all thy heart and with all thy soul.

Proverbs 8:17

I love them that love me; and those that seek me early shall find me.

Jeremiah 29:13

And ye shall seek me, and find me, when ye shall search for me with all your heart.

Matthew 7:7

Ask, and it shall be given you; seek, and ye shall find; knock, and it shall be opened unto you:

Matthew 7:8

For every one that asketh receiveth; and he that seeketh findeth; and to him that knocketh it shall be opened.

Reading these verses is refreshing to the heart, now let us look at chapter 2 of proverbs and I will draw your attention to verses 4-7

If thou seekest her as silver, and searchest for her as for hid treasures;

Then shalt thou understand the fear of the Lord, and find the knowledge of God.

For the Lord giveth wisdom: out of his mouth cometh knowledge and understanding.

He layeth up sound wisdom for the righteous: he is a buckler to them that walk uprightly.

I know as women we are all looking for ways of providing for our families and that is basically why everyone goes to work, its to get some goods or services in exchange for your money but should we seek for money more than seeking the Lord? No. As we have seen there are some things we need in life like security and trust that is so rare in our world today but is in abundance when we seek the Lord first and that is what these verses above are about. Even beauty is not something we should seek for first before we have sought and found the Wisdom of God who is Christ Jesus, because only then do we understand the reverential and worshipful fear of the Lord which we need to be an ideal woman, remember that is our focus; to be the Designer's best and bring out the uniqueness that is in you as a woman who the Lord God designed. The Lord is the giver of wisdom and He told us in James 1:5 we should ask and He will give us.

If any of you lack wisdom, let him ask of God, that giveth to all men liberally, and upbraideth not; and it shall be given him.

It is interesting that the Lord tells us to embrace the Wisdom of God and it will lead us to reverencing Him and worshipfully fear Him as the key basically to be the woman He made us to be, I would like you to read with me if you will the following verses found in proverbs chapter 3. I think many women do not have the right foundation of their inner selves and as women if we get hold of this principle and just embrace the Lord Jesus Christ. The amplified version of the bible writes the 13th verse of proverbs 13 like this;

Happy (blessed, fortunate, and enviable) is the man who finds skillful and Godly Wisdom, and the man who gets understanding [drawing it forth from God's Word and life's experiences].

So any woman who gets Godly Wisdom is blessed, happy she is fortunate and enviable, hallelujah! Wisdom of God also has wonderful rewards that are so exciting to read about which again cannot be bought and so are priceless and as you read these verses below you will definitely realize that but just to list them we have: long life, riches, honor, peace and pleasant ways, what a blessing it is to find Christ Jesus. Let us read the rest of the verses in this chapter please;

Happy is the man that findeth wisdom, and the man that getteth understanding.

For the merchandise of it is better than the merchandise of silver, and the gain thereof than fine gold.

She is more precious than rubies: and all the things thou canst desire are not to be compared unto her.

Length of days is in her right hand; and in her left hand riches and honour.

Her ways are ways of pleasantness, and all her paths are peace.

She is a tree of life to them that lay hold upon her: and happy is every one that retaineth her.

The Lord by wisdom hath founded the earth; by understanding hath he established the heavens.

Do you remember the tree of life in the Garden of Eden? Did you know that its fruits will be eaten in some time to come? Well verse 18 tells us who it is, sometimes I wonder if only Adam and Eve had eaten it before they sinned they would not have been tricked and so there would be no death, wow! Can you imagine that? The good news is they didn't eat it after they sinned. Let's see more on the tree of life and what the Word of God says about it,

Proverbs 11:30

The fruit of the righteous is a tree of life; and he that winneth souls is wise.

Proverbs 13:12

Hope deferred maketh the heart sick: but when the desire cometh, it is a tree of life.

Proverbs 15:4

A wholesome tongue is a tree of life: but perverseness therein is a breach in the spirit.

Revelation 2:7

He that hath an ear let him hear what the Spirit saith unto the churches; To him that overcometh will I give to eat of the tree of life, which is in the midst of the paradise of God.

Revelation 22:2

In the midst of the street of it, and on either side of the river, was there the tree of life, which bare twelve manner of fruits, and yielded her fruit every month: and the leaves of the tree were for the healing of the nations.

Revelation 22:14

Blessed are they that do his commandments, that they

may have right to the tree of life, and may enter in through the gates into the city.

THE TREASURES OF WISDOM

All treasures of wisdom are in Christ Jesus our Lord that is the only place we can find them; in Him
Colossians 2: 2-3

That their hearts might be comforted, being knit together in love, and unto all riches of the full assurance of understanding, to the acknowledgment of the mystery of God, and of the Father, and of Christ; in whom are hid all the treasures of wisdom and knowledge.
Isaiah 45:3
And I will give thee the treasures of darkness, and hidden riches of secret places, that thou mayest know that I, the LORD, which call thee by thy name, am the God of Israel.

How much should we value Wisdom? The 8th verse of proverbs chapter 4 tells us to prize Wisdom highly and we should exalt her. The following verses in this chapter will give us the treasures of Wisdom in fact just reading these verses paints such a beautiful and lovely picture of our Lord Jesus

Christ and all He has for us as women in the 21st century please read them with me would you?

Proverbs 4: 6-13

Forsake her not, and she shall preserve thee: love her, and she shall keep thee.

Wisdom is the principal thing; therefore get wisdom: and with all thy getting get understanding.

Exalt her, and she shall promote thee: she shall bring thee to honour, when thou dost embrace her.

She shall give to thine head an ornament of grace: a crown of glory shall she deliver to thee.

Hear, O my son, and receive my sayings; and the years of thy life shall be many.

I have taught thee in the way of wisdom; I have led thee in right paths.

When thou goest, thy steps shall not be straitened; and when thou runnest, thou shalt not stumble.

Take fast hold of instruction; let her not go: keep her; for she is thy life.

If we walk in obedience to the Lord and embrace Wisdom this is what we should expect:

- ❖ Wisdom will keep you
- ❖ Defend you
- ❖ Protect you

- ❖ Guard you
- ❖ Exalt you
- ❖ Promote you
- ❖ Honor you
- ❖ Crown you with beauty and glory
- ❖ Give you grace
- ❖ Give you long life

Isn't this what any woman would want? I sure would want all of this in my life, would you?

This is what the Wisdom of God who is Christ Jesus our Lord tells us about himself in the 8th chapter of proverbs, read with me these powerful verses, will you please?

The fear of the Lord is to hate evil: pride, and arrogancy, and the evil way, and the froward mouth, do I hate.

Counsel is mine, and sound wisdom: I am understanding; I have strength.

By me kings reign, and princes decree justice.

By me princes rule, and nobles, even all the judges of the earth.

I love them that love me; and those that seek me early shall find me.

Riches and honour are with me; yea, durable riches and righteousness.

My fruit is better than gold, yea, than fine gold; and my

revenue than choice silver.

I lead in the way of righteousness, in the midst of the paths of judgment:

That I may cause those that love me to inherit substance; and I will fill their treasures.

The Lord possessed me in the beginning of his way, before his works of old.

I was set up from everlasting, from the beginning, or ever the earth was.

When there were no depths, I was brought forth; when there were no fountains abounding with water.

Before the mountains were settled, before the hills was I brought forth:

While as yet he had not made the earth, nor the fields, nor the highest part of the dust of the world.

When he prepared the heavens, I was there: when he set a compass upon the face of the depth:

When he established the clouds above: when he strengthened the fountains of the deep:

When he gave to the sea his decree, that the waters should not pass his commandment: when he appointed the foundations of the earth:

Then I was by him, as one brought up with him: and I was daily his delight, rejoicing always before him;

Rejoicing in the habitable part of his earth; and my delights were with the sons of men.

Now therefore hearken unto me, O ye children: for blessed are they that keep my ways.

Hear instruction, and be wise, and refuse it not.

Blessed is the man that heareth me, watching daily at my gates, waiting at the posts of my doors.

For whoso findeth me findeth life, and shall obtain favour of the Lord.

But he that sinneth against me wrongeth his own soul: all they that hate me love death.

Isn't this the perfect picture of our Lord Jesus Christ? The Lord Holy Spirit revealed Christ to king Solomon through these proverbs. The bible tells us that the Word of God is inspired by God.

2Timothy 3:16

All scripture is given by inspiration of God, and is profitable for doctrine, for reproof, for correction, for instruction in righteousness:

The Word of God cannot be compared to anything in this world if you hide it in your heart nothing will stop you from being the original, unique designed woman that the Lord created. You will be able to fulfill the purpose of God for you life here on earth. There is no love greater than the Love of God and that is all a woman wants; unconditional love, you want to be loved and not feel used or dirty but clean and lovely all the time from the time you knew no man sexually until the time you knew a man sexually, you want to be told you are beautiful whether you are 16 or 99 years of age, you want to be loved when your moods are low and when they are high, when you feel down or up.

Can you imagine a girl who was raped or sexually molested by a parent or relative or even a stranger? Doesn't she want to feel clean and accepted and not condemned, but loved just like a girl who is married a virgin to the man she prayed for and grew up in a loving home would feel? They are both women with the same needs but in different circumstances. Ok let me bring it closer home, maybe it will make more sense; a young girl born in a war torn country would like to walk down the aisle in a white gown, then go for her honey moon to a fancy hotel beach somewhere and then come home to her house and bring up her children, care for her husband and do all that her heart desires to do but then finds herself in a refugee camp with several men not well groomed who are so poor and the only hope is where will the next meal come from. That is one scenario while there is another one who is also a young girl but with no parents, another is a young girl will a good family and no problems so life is different to all of us but our feelings and requirements as women are the same no matter your background or culture. There is something all women can have that is of the same quality and that is life in Jesus Christ and His unfailing and unconditional love. That is why my passion is to know Him with all I have and all I am, because without Him I am nothing. If we women get together and do our God given duty, we will change the world because we are the ones who bring up human beings in this world, we are the mothers, we are the only ones God has given the responsibility to bring forth life, lets be good custodians of this privilege.

A WOMAN IN GOD'S EYES

God is love and He loves us all, He is our creator the bible tells us He created us both male and female in His image; that is why He sent His only Son our Lord Jesus Christ to die for us. Our heavenly father loves us unconditionally with an eternal love and nothing can separate us from the love of God.

Romans 8:39

Nor height, nor depth, nor any other creature, shall be able to separate us from the love of God, which is in Christ Jesus our Lord.

2 Thessalonians 2:16

Now our Lord Jesus Christ himself, and God, even our Father, which hath loved us, and hath given us everlasting consolation and good hope through grace,

John 16:27

For the Father himself loveth you, because ye have loved me, and have believed that I came out from God.

We are confident from the Word of God that He loves us. Yes God loves you. So today if you feel not loved or if you have a different picture of God in your mind as many people do that, He is strict and ready to punish you then you need to change and renew your thinking with these scriptures and know today that God loves you; yes you. It doesn't matter what you have done in the past or even a few minutes ago or what you will do later on; God still loves you. Take a moment and think about it, talk to yourself and think of the love of God for you not for someone else but just for you.

Can I share a testimony about myself with you? I had the wrong concept of God in my mind and thought He didn't love me as much as He loved others because my mother died and left me when I was 19 years old and then I later got into depression and bottled up anger. I had such a low self esteem that made me such a pessimist in life that I didn't do well in my bachelor's degree. This then made things worse for me because

I felt worthless and useless thinking that I had wasted a brilliant mind the Lord had given me. But the good news is it all changed when I got this revelation of the love of God for me from the Lord Holy Spirit. I know He can do it again and again for anyone who reads this book and was like me, if God did it for me He will do it for you today.

When I got this realization of the love of God for me it changed the way I think about God and myself. Nowadays when I have a problem, or treated unjustly by someone, I know that its not a way of God trying to punish me but that He loves me and will help me go through and solve the problem. I pray that you get this same revelation today as you read about the love of God for us. In fact if you are having a low self esteem or do not have self love this is what I would recommend you do with these scriptures it worked for me and I know it will work out for you; take all of these scriptures and where it is written 'you or us or our' put your name there and then read the verse aloud to yourself not once or twice but everyday until you start having self worth and strength within you that God loves you and that God is not out to punish you for the wrongs you did in life. Keep on doing this until these scriptures are living in your heart and whenever the thought of condemnation comes to you then you can take the scripture from your heart and say it aloud to cancel the negative thought. I have done this myself and today no one can tell me that God doesn't love me, no one; I know that I know beyond knowing that God loves me and nothing can separate me from His love I am His and He is mine for ever. So when I miss the mark one day and fall I get right up and repent of my sin then continue in the love of God, the bible says the afflictions of the righteous are many but He delivers us from them all [Psalms 34:19 Many are the afflictions of the righteous: but the LORD delivereth him out of them all.] and in Proverbs it says; [Proverbs 24:16

For a just man falleth seven times, and riseth up again: but the wicked shall fall into mischief.] Read these scriptures with me again and meditate on them everyday as you walk in the love of God;

Romans 5:5

And hope maketh not ashamed; because the love of God is shed abroad in our hearts by the Holy Ghost which is given unto us.

Romans 5:8

But God commendeth his love toward us, in that, while we were yet sinners, Christ died for us.

Galatians 2:20

I am crucified with Christ: neverthless I live; yet not I, but

Christ liveth in me: and the life which I now live in the flesh I live by the faith of the Son of God, who loved me, and gave himself for me.

Ephesians 2:4

But God, who is rich in mercy, for his great love wherewith he loved us,

Ephesians 3:19

And to know the love of Christ, which passeth knowledge, that ye might be filled with all the fulness of God.

1 John 2:5

But whoso keepeth his word, in him verily is the love of God perfected: hereby know we that we are in him.

1 John 4:9

In this was manifested the love of God toward us, because that God sent his only begotten Son into the world, that we might live through him.

1 John 4:10

Herein is love, not that we loved God, but that he loved us, and sent his Son to be the propitiation for our sins.

1 John 4:11

Beloved, if God so loved us, we ought also to love one another.

1 John 4:12

No man hath seen God at any time. If we love one

another, God dwelleth in us, and his love is perfected in us.

1 John 4:16

And we have known and believed the love that God hath to us. God is love; and he that dwelleth in love dwelleth in God, and God in him.

1 John 5:3

For this is the love of God, that we keep his commandments: and his commandments are not grievous.

What did the Lord have in mind when He created a woman? This is a good question to answer and a good place to start that will give us a purpose and reason to why we are the way we are as women. Whenever my husband and I buy some equipment, I insist on reading the manual first before operating it and most if not all the times I learn something I didn't know about the equipment we bought that I thought was obvious, so in the same way as a woman I need to read the manual from the manufacturer Himself who made me and all women to understand how we are supposed to work and operate efficiently in this world we live in, don't you think so? Ok then let's look at what the Lord God who is the Original designer of women says about them.

Alright let us start with who created a woman and from what? God Almighty created a woman and He created her from a man's rib. Who named a woman? The man called Adam did. Why didn't God name the woman? A very good question let us look at the following verses for the answer;

Genesis 1:27

So God created man in his own image, in the image of God created he him; male and female created he them.

Genesis 1:28

And God blessed them, and God said unto them, be fruitful, and multiply, and replenish the earth, and subdue it: and have dominion over the fish of the sea, and over the fowl of the air, and over every living thing that moveth upon the earth.

Genesis 1:31

And God saw every thing that he had made, and, behold, it was very good. And the evening and the morning were the sixth day.

Genesis 2:7

And the Lord God formed man of the dust of the ground, and breathed into his nostrils the breath of life; and man became a living soul.

Genesis 2:18

And the Lord God said, It is not good that the man should be alone; I will make him an help meet for him.

Genesis 2:20- 25

And Adam gave names to all cattle, and to the fowl of the air, and to every beast of the field; but for Adam there was not found an help meet for him. And the Lord God caused a deep sleep to fall upon Adam, and he slept: and he took one of his ribs, and closed up the flesh instead thereof; and the rib, which the Lord God had taken from man, made he a woman, and brought her unto the man. And Adam said, This is now bone of my bones, and flesh of my flesh: she shall be called Woman, because she was taken out of Man. Therefore shall a man leave his father and his mother, and shall cleave unto his wife: and they shall be one flesh. And they were both naked, the man and his wife, and were not ashamed.

Ok please be patient with me and follow this carefully and by the end of this trip in these verses you will know who you are as a woman in Christ, ok lets get going, from these verses we see that God created them both in His image but then you will notice in Genesis chapter 2 it is written that the woman is made out of the man's rib so what is going on here? Is this a contradiction? No it is not, let me explain it to you as the Lord Holy Spirit taught me this is what happened:

On the sixth day both were created by the Lord God but the process is what is being explained in chapter 2. So Adam was made out of the dust of the ground as you have read in Genesis 2:7 and then the woman was created from the man's rib as you read in Genesis 2:21. The Lord then introduced her to the man and that is why Adam named her woman not Eve. Woman means; taken out of the man. So all this happened on the sixth day and then the Lord blessed them and gave them dominion over all the earth that is in Genesis 1:28 and they were all very good that is what the Lord said in verse 31 of the same chapter.

Did you know that Adam renamed his wife a second time? Oh yes she was not called Eve, in the beginning. Eve means 'life' and Woman means 'out of a man' that is a big difference, I had never seen that until the Lord Holy Spirit showed it to me, the first time she was called Eve was in the 3rd chapter of Genesis;

Genesis 3:20-21

And Adam called his wife's name Eve; because she was the mother of all living. Unto Adam also and to his wife did the Lord God make coats of skins, and clothed them.

She was renamed to Eve after the fall that is after they had sinned against God and so now she was going to be the mother of the whole human race. Have you noticed that now they are clothed and before they were naked and not ashamed? I thought I should slide that in, interesting isn't it? Sin exposes you while the righteousness of God clothes you.

I would like to mention here that there were consequences to Eve because of the sin they committed and it is a biblical statement that the man will rule over the woman and she will have pain or labor when having her children. I believe the Lord said this with love towards women because God is love.

Genesis 3:16

Unto the woman he said, I will greatly multiply thy sorrow and thy conception; in sorrow thou shalt bring forth children; and thy desire shall be to thy husband, and he shall rule over thee.

I hope you enjoyed the trip of knowing yourself up to this point, alright the other important question to ask is, what was the purpose for a woman? What does the Lord say about this?

She was to be a suitable helper to the man we get this in the verses above in Genesis chapter 2.

A woman therefore is a person who should give help to the man in any area he needs help in. She is the only suitable help for a man the Lord must have built her for this very purpose. In the ministry of Christ and even in Paul's ministry you see women helping out in the ministry they didn't fight for positions no, they helped in all positions. Remember the Lord blessed them both man and woman and gave dominion over the earth to both but with different roles, we will talk more on roles later. There are things that only a woman can do best and there are others that only a man can do best. The point here is men and women shouldn't be competing they should be augmenting each other. That is a big difference, when people are competing they are trying to out smart the other and that is wrong men and women are suppose to work together in unison then the whole purpose of life would work out very well. This also applies to marriages when spouses start competing then the marriage fails because then one person feels inferior to the other but when they are working together to better one another then they make a force that even the devil cannot challenge. That is why the Lord said that is why a man shall leave his mother and father and cleave to his wife. Do you know what cleave means? It means to stick together like with glue; and that is why He says then they will become one not they will become two no one. My dear friend if you are married you need to glue to your husband and become one with him and he also has to be the leader or the head of the home. When this order is corrected in a marriage it always works.

What amazed me about our Lord Jesus is that in His ministry he went out of His way especially in those days where the custom was for women to sit back and they did not interact with men that much but the Lord kept on including them in His ministry this tells us something as women that the Lord cares to interact with us in a personal way. He even went to visit Mary and Martha and while Martha was busy complaining Mary was busy enjoying the Lord and listening to the Word of God. It is not bad to be someone who likes making the visitors comfortable but you have to learn how to balance where when someone like Jesus the Son of God visits you that is not the time to prepare food you can do that later after listening to the word. The Word of God is the bread of life and no one can live without it but food you can stay without if for days and you will still be living. We can learn something from that do not be too preoccupied with the things of this world until you forget the main reason you are living; we live for Christ, we belong to Him, He is the one who paid the price for us to live an abundant life so let us try to keep the weeds out of the gardens of our heart by listening to the word of God and filling our hearts with it. Something we as women should learn from this passage below is that we should learn to listen to the Word of God and not be so busy ministering to others and forget we also need the Word. Look at this;

Luke 10:38- 42

Now it came to pass, as they went, that he entered into a certain village: and a certain woman named Martha received him into her house. And she had a sister called Mary, which also sat at Jesus' feet, and heard his word. But Martha was cumbered about much serving, and came to him, and said, Lord, dost thou not care that my sister hath left me to serve alone? bid her therefore that she help me.

And Jesus answered and said unto her, Martha, Martha, thou art careful and troubled about many things: but one thing is needful: and Mary hath chosen that good part, which shall not be taken away from her.

Luke 7:37

And, behold, a woman in the city, which was a sinner, when she knew that Jesus sat at meat in the Pharisee's house, brought an alabaster box of ointment,

Luke 7:39

Now when the Pharisee which had bidden him saw it, he spake within himself, saying, This man, if he were a prophet, would have known who and what manner of woman this is that toucheth him: for she is a sinner.
Luke 7:44

And he turned to the woman, and said unto Simon, Seest thou this woman? I entered into thine house, thou gavest me no water for my feet: but she hath washed my feet with tears, and wiped them with the hairs of her head.
Luke 7:45

Thou gavest me no kiss: but this woman since the time I came in hath not ceased to kiss my feet.
Luke 7:46

My head with oil thou didst not anoint: but this woman hath anointed my feet with ointment.
Luke 7:50

And he said to the woman, Thy faith hath saved thee; go in peace.

The verses above trigger a question in my mind for 21st century women and it is this; how much do you value Christ Jesus in your life can you do what this woman did and anoint the Lord with your praise for Him because that is basically what she did she was praising the Lord and worshiping Him. She poured an expensive perfume at His feet that maybe she had saved a whole year to buy! Are you a career woman too busy to set aside valuable time with your maker? She saw something that no one saw in Christ in that whole room; she saw her Savoir, her Redeemer who would cleanse her of all the things she had done in her life. Sometimes most women are busy doing their modern lifestyle activities and forget their Designer and then when everything starts falling apart you wonder what happened. This is a challenge to modern day women to seek their first love with the Lord and give Him quality time, do not pray when you are in trouble but rather put the trouble away from coming by being a prayerful woman. Esther was a queen but she fasted for 3 days to seek the Lord and get favor to save her people. She had just won a beauty contest maybe something like miss universe or something like that and she had the time to intercede and fast, that should challenge us, career women. Life is not all about beauty there is more to life than that.

Can I give you another testimony about myself concerning this issue? I never knew there was much more in life than just loving, beauty, dancing and having fun or what I thought was fun. But when I met Christ not religiously but I mean knowing God intimately by reading His word, studying it and praying, depending on the Lord Holy Spirit for everything in my life, I mean total dependence on the Lord. Then life started changing

I tell you my self esteem as I shared earlier improved dramatically, my physical body changed and looked better, my marriage became wonderful and life now is so precious to me because I no longer live but Christ who loved me enough to die for me is the one living in me, He is my hope and my life. I pray in the name of Jesus that you will come to this level in your life where you live a higher life not just ordinary life but supernatural life where you talk with your maker or yes you have a face to face encounter daily with the Lord. And every second He is guiding you in all you do and is with you, I cannot tell you how beautiful and free that feels especially when things are so unpredictable nowadays but just to know the maker of heaven and earth is your father and He loves you and is working for you and so no one or nothing can be against you, I wish I could put what I feel in writing its just that is to wonderful a feeling to put in words only if you walk in it will you appreciate what I mean here and I pray that you will live this higher life in Christ once you accept Him and allow Him to manage and be owner of your life.

There are many Samaritan women in the 21st century and most of them are working women or as they could be called career women. I would like to talk to the woman who may be reading this book and you are fed up of sexual relationships, oh yes; I mean you feel used, unappreciated, useless, worthless, cheated and of no value at all because, you have failed in each relationship you have tried out. There are women who are married and have these feeling welling up in them some are even Christian women but they have these feelings. You have been married and this is the nth time, divorced and remarried, separated and remarried, living together and then separated; name it and you have gone through it. One abortion after another trying to get the right man to marry you correcting one wrong with another wrong but he never seems to work. Maybe you have been a hooker or worked for a drug dealer, whatever a woman can do to get money maybe you have done it all. One make over after the other trying to look younger all the time and up to the latest fashion but still the men don't seem to stay on, well you may feel alone but you are not alone, Jesus loves you and while you were still doing all that He died for you and paid the price of that sin on your behalf all you need to do now is to accept that sacrifice He made for you and let Him own you and live in you. There is hope and a new beginning only that this time one that will never fail. If He did it for the Samaritan woman wouldn't He do it for you? He sure will just trust Him, He loves you so much that Jesus said no one will ever separate you from His love that includes no thing. It may not be you but maybe someone you know has gone through all this and even maybe much more and people have given up and now have a nickname because of the unfortunate circumstances surrounding her, maybe you can encourage someone like that with these verses below because God has a plan for each one of us, I know you must be asking, you mean even for such a woman as you have described? Yes even for her or even worse God is no respector of persons and nothing is new to Him, the Lord has a plan just look at the story of the Samaritan woman, I mean she ended up being an evangelist to her community, the Lord used her to preach to them who the Messiah was and they received eternal life!! Doesn't that sound like a good plan the Lord had for her and as it says in Jeremiah 29:11- thoughts of good and not of evil towards His children? It sounds so to me. He shows no partiality what He does for one He will do for the other, so I have got news to all women who have no marriages, no love to look forward to from a man, messed up by life issues there is hope in Jesus Christ and He will do it for you as He did it for the Samaritan woman, yes Jesus loves you just the way you are, hallelujah!

Who knows what made this woman marry seven times? I sure don't know why but I have done psychology and may try to imagine some of the reasons why- maybe she was sexually abused as a child by a parent or relative that could be a possibility or maybe she was raped by some stranger when coming from school or the market place or she was an orphan and had no where else to go and so looked for love in sexual relationships, I mean I could go on and on but I certainly don't know the reason apart from what I can read in the bible and it seems she was so ashamed of herself, her self esteem and self worth was so low that she could not walk with other women and fetch water together, she was actually a loner. Could that be you? If it is then do not worry because Christ is the answer and a permanent answer this time.

Please read these verses with me, will you please?

John 4:7

There cometh a woman of Samaria to draw water: Jesus saith unto her, Give me to drink.

John 4:9

Then saith the woman of Samaria unto him, How is it that thou, being a Jew, askest drink of me, which am a woman of Samaria? for the Jews have no dealings with the Samaritans.

John 4:11

The woman saith unto him, Sir, thou hast nothing to draw with, and the well is deep: from whence then hast thou that living water?

John 4:15

The woman saith unto him, Sir, give me this water, that I

thirst not, neither come hither to draw.

John 4:17

The woman answered and said, I have no husband. Jesus said unto her, Thou hast well said, I have no husband:

John 4:19

The woman saith unto him, Sir, I perceive that thou art a prophet.

John 4:21

Jesus saith unto her, Woman, believe me, the hour cometh, when ye shall neither in this mountain, nor yet at Jerusalem, worship the Father.

John 4:25

The woman saith unto him, I know that Messias cometh, which is called Christ: when he is come, he will tell us all things.

John 4:27-28

And upon this came his disciples, and marvelled that he talked with the woman: yet no man said, What seekest thou? or, Why talkest thou with her? The woman then left her waterpot, and went her way into the city, and saith to the men,

John 4:39

And many of the Samaritans of that city believed on him for the saying of the woman, which testified, He told me all that ever I did.

John 4:42

And said unto the woman, Now we believe, not because of thy saying: for we have heard him ourselves, and know that this is indeed the Christ, the Saviour of the world.

Sometimes the society condemns and looks down upon those they refer as misfits, but the misfits or victims of circumstances as it were have hope in the Kingdom of God and that is good news. If you are a woman who has missed the point or it may not be you who missed the point but a friend or a loved one that you know it doesn't matter what people call you or the person you know it maybe they will call her a prostitute, husband snatcher, loose woman, used woman whatever the name may be remember Christ Jesus does not condemn such women in His eyes they are His daughters and so if you are reading this book and these names ring a bell in your memories take heart because Jesus loves you and calls you daughter, have a look at these scriptures:

John 8:3

And the scribes and Pharisees brought unto him a woman taken in adultery; and when they had set her in the midst,

John 8:4

They say unto him, Master, this woman was taken in adultery, in the very act.

John 8:9

And they which heard it, being convicted by their own conscience, went out one by one, beginning at the eldest, even unto the last: and Jesus was left alone, and the woman standing in the midst.

John 8:10

When Jesus had lifted up himself, and saw none but the woman, he said unto her, Woman, where are those thine accusers? hath no man condemned thee?

Sometimes we live in a world where only bad news are given a voice but not much of good news to hear well did you know it was women who first went to the tomb? Its amazing the kind of love women have for the Lord you can see it through out the bible and even in churches or meeting today most attendees are women. There were faithful women who served the Lord or even servants of the Lord that is what is special about a faithful ideal woman she loves the Lord all the way. We are His daughters, have you ever seen a young daughter with her father? You see her all over the dad lavishing him with love and kisses isn't it? I think you get the picture. Women were created to nurture and to love and comfort.

John 20:13

And they say unto her, Woman, why weepest thou? She saith unto them, Because they have taken away my

LORD, and I know not where they have laid him.
John 20:15
Jesus saith unto her, Woman, why weepest thou? whom seekest thou? She, supposing him to be the gardener, saith unto him, Sir, if thou have borne him hence, tell me where thou hast laid him, and I will take him away.

In the ministry of Paul there were women who heard the gospel and got saved in fact some of the people who heard the gospel and were among the first to get saved were women. I know there are controversial subjects on women in ministry to the Lord but here we see they were involved in Paul's ministry and most of all in the ministry of our Lord Jesus Christ. This is an example for women to serve and work for the Lord.

Acts 9:36
Now there was at Joppa a certain disciple named Tabitha, which by interpretation is called Dorcas: this woman was full of good works and alms deeds which she did.
Acts 16:14
And a certain woman named Lydia, a seller of purple, of the city of Thyatira, which worshipped God, heard us: whose heart the Lord opened, that she attended unto the things which were spoken of Paul.
Acts 17:34

Howbeit certain men clave unto him, and believed: among the which was Dionysius the Areopagite, and a woman named Damaris, and others with them.

GOD GIVEN ROLES FOR A WOMAN

In both old and new testaments women have had several roles to play in the community and world history some roles have been negative and others positive of course we are looking for the positive ones. As said earlier in this book that there are many Old and New Testament ideal women and even here, as we talk on the roles of a woman we will see some of these women and their roles in the bible, I will sight a number of them. Before I do that I would like to say here that these are not the only roles of a woman they are just a few of what we can sight from the bible. We live in the 21st century where there has been a lot of development and increase in technology since bible days so I am not saying women can only do what I will be talking about I just want women to get the foundation of what the Lord has purposed as the role of women in general. Like in bible days there were no airplanes so does that mean women cannot be pilots or work in the airlines? Of course not! You see what I mean? Remember women are in the image of God so keep that in mind as you read the roles below.

Of course the major role of a woman as we have seen in the book of Genesis is to:

- Bring forth children and care for them. It is from this role that we have great men of God like Prophet Samuel, John the Baptist, the Messiah our Lord Jesus Christ, Samson and many others.

- Be a helper to her husband

- They can be prophetesses as He did use Miriam, Deborah, Huldah and Anna. Even today we have women of God being used by Him as prophetesses.

Exodus 15:20
And Miriam the prophetess, the sister of Aaron, took a timbrel in her hand; and all the women went out after her with timbrels and with dances.
Esther 2:17
And the king loved Esther above all the women, and she obtained grace and favour in his sight more than all the virgins; so that he set the royal crown upon her head, and made her queen instead of Vashti.
Judges 4:4
And Deborah, a prophetess, the wife of Lapidoth, she

judged Israel at that time.

2 Kings 22:14

So Hilkiah the priest, and Ahikam, and Achbor, and Shaphan, and Asahiah, went unto Huldah the prophetess, the wife of Shallum the son of Tikvah, the son of Harhas, keeper of the wardrobe; (now she dwelt in Jerusalem in the college;) and they communed with her.

Luke 2:36

And there was one Anna, a prophetess, the daughter of Phanuel, of the tribe of Aser: she was of a great age, and had lived with an husband seven years from her virginity;

- Leaders both spiritual and national

Acts 16:14

One of them was Lydia from Thyatira, a merchant of expensive purple cloth. She was a worshiper of God. As she listened to us, the Lord opened her heart, and she accepted what Paul was saying.

Proverbs 31:18-24

She perceiveth that her merchandise is good: her candle goeth not out by night.

She layeth her hands to the spindle, and her hands hold the distaff.

*She stretcheth out her hand to the poor; yea, she reacheth forth her hands to the
needy.*

She is not afraid of the snow for her household: for all her household are clothed with scarlet.

She maketh herself coverings of tapestry; her clothing is silk and purple.

Her husband is known in the gates, when he sitteth among the elders of the land.

She maketh fine linen, and selleth it; and delivereth girdles unto the merchant.

Titus 2:3-5

The aged women likewise, that they be in behaviour as becometh holiness, not false accusers, not given to much wine, teachers of good things; that they may teach the young women to be sober, to love their husbands, to love their children, to be discreet, chaste, keepers at home, good, obedient to their own husbands, that the word of God be not blasphemed.

These are some of the virtues we see that are God given to women from the scriptures above they can be good;

- Teachers
- Managers
- Entrepreneurs
- Organizers
- Marketers
- Home makers

THE BEAUTY OF A WOMAN

Physical beauty is not all that a woman is, there is inner beauty which is superior to outside beauty. We still need to use all the technology out there to keep our bodies looking good like all the anti aging medicine that is there today but still its not possible to look 16 years of age when you are 70 so no matter what you do as a woman your physical body will change. Of course we should keep the temple of our Lord which is our body well and fit which includes using the anti aging medicine tips, exercises, relaxation therapies and all that but that should not be all it is to you as a woman. That shouldn't be your self worth, your value should be how Christ sees you and so developing holiness and purity by walking in the fear of the Lord is what really matters. So with that in mind then the following verse will help.

Proverbs 31:30

Favour is deceitful, and beauty is vain: but a woman that feareth the LORD, she shall be praised.

1 Timothy 2:9(NLT)

And I want women to be modest in their appearance. They should wear decent and appropriate clothing and not draw attention to themselves by the way they fix their hair or by wearing gold or pearls or expensive clothes.

1 Timothy 2:15(NLT)

But women will be saved through childbearing and by continuing to live in faith, love, holiness, and modesty.

Looking at our society today it seems to me at least that nudity is the key to beauty, I am sorry if I am stepping on your toes with this subject but please listen me out please I do not mean to offend anyone with this issue I just want us to read the bible and see what it says about women and how they should respect their bodies. So I tend to disagree with the idea of nudity being the key to beauty I think a woman can be clothed and look exceptionally beautiful. Please do not take me wrong here, I like fashion, I mean a woman needs to look beautiful physically so I am not saying do not put on make up or have nice designed dresses or smell good but what I am saying is, a woman's breast do not need to be outside for her to look beautiful or her behind doesn't need to be visible to the public for us to know she is female! Our body is for the Lord in fact the bible says it is the Lord's temple so how can we treat it like that? Ask yourself this questions each time you dress, would I dress like this and go and meet Christ? Does this outfit honor the Lord? If yes then wear it.

1 Corinthians 6:19

Or don't you know that your body is the temple of the Holy Spirit, who lives in you and was given to you by God? You do not belong to yourself,

Another issue that is so common is sex before marriage opps! Here I am again sorry I hope I am not offending you with this either. The bible calls having sex before marriage -fornication and extra marital affairs that, the bible calls adultery. As a wife you don't have to have sex with someone who is not your husband to show your love and commitment, there are other ways apart from sex that one can show commitment and love in a relationship outside of marriage. In Africa for example where I come from improper sexual activity has killed millions of people with AIDS and left millions of children as orphans. Is 5 minutes of pleasure worth life? I know nowadays sex has been made to look like this unusual experience that is almost out of this world and so everyone has this chemical reaction that happens in their body that is not controllable, making it the cool thing to do among the youth and yet it's a lie. Its through sex that one gets pregnant without planning to, gets Sexually transmitted diseases some that are fatal and some that can be treated, not to mention the spiritual impurity that one gets themselves into and the psychological effects of sex out of marriage especially for women; most people are not told of these consequences of sex. The bible says my people perish for lack of knowledge. Getting knowledge about something before doing it is very important, it can save a life. Sex in its proper place which is in the marriage is very good, it is a precious gift in marriage.

I do not mean to offend anyone with this I just would like women to think of their bodies as a temple for the Lord. And to know that the Lord Holy Spirit is living in us who are born again, have a look at these verses;

1 Corinthians 6:18-20

Flee fornication. Every sin that a man doeth is without the body; but he that committeth

fornication sinneth against his own body. What? know ye not that your body is the temple

of the Holy Ghost which is in you, which ye have of God, and ye are not your own? For

ye are bought with a price: therefore glorify God in your body, and in your spirit, which are God's.

1 Timothy 4:12

Let no man despise thy youth; but be thou an example of the believers, in word, in conversation, in charity, in spirit, in faith, in purity.

1 Timothy 5:2

The elder women as mothers; the younger as sisters, with all purity.

1 Corinthians 7:2

Nevertheless, to avoid fornication, let every man have his own wife, and let every woman have her own husband.

WIVES

A Wife is a treasure that the Lord has given any man that finds one. The bible tells us that a wife is a fruitful vine and will flourish in her home. This means that a wife can make a home prosperous and a place full of productivity. It is the wife that sets the mood in the home, a happy and joyful wife will have a happy and joyful family. Have you ever noticed that when the wife is frustrated and stressed in the house then everyone seems to have the same mood; the children and husband become cranky and unfriendly? It's as if stress from the mother is contagious. Its because the mother is to be the fruitful vine of the home and make it flourish.

Proverbs 18:22

The man who finds a wife finds a treasure and receives favor from the Lord.

Psalms 128:3-4

Your wife will be like a fruitful vine, flourishing within your home. And look at all those children! There they sit around your table as vigorous and healthy as young olive trees. That is the Lord's reward for those who fear him.

Marriage is good and it's blessed by the Lord in fact it was the Lord's idea to have a man and wife as we see in the book of Genesis that God created both male and female and the woman was a suitable helper to the man and so the first marriage was between Adam and Eve notice there was only one Eve! And we don't read anywhere in the bible where Adam abused Eve physically by punching her or kicking her or even hitting her, the bible says a man who loves his wife loves himself. This is because the woman came out of the man they are one when they get married. A marriage should be kept pure and honorable that is what the Word of God instructs us. Which means that it can be contaminated with things like; adultery, disrespect, competition, envy and jealousy just mentioning a few.

Hebrews 13:4

Marriage is honourable in all, and the bed undefiled: but whoremongers and adulterers God will judge.

A marriage can only work if its based on love and not lust. This is the definition of love according to the bible;

1 Corinthians 13:4-8

Love is patient and kind. Love is not jealous or boastful or proud or rude. Love does not demand its own way. Love is not irritable, and it keeps no record of when it has been wronged. It is never glad about injustice but rejoices whenever the truth wins out. Love never gives up, never loses faith, is always hopeful, and endures through every circumstance.

Love will last forever, but prophecy and speaking in unknown languages and special knowledge will all disappear.

The Word of the Lord has good advice for married women. Marriage works it is a wonderful union the Lord has given to the human race. Marriage can only be stressful without Christ but in Christ it's a wonderful and dependable union. There is one issue though that most women in the 21st century do not like hearing, which is submission. This is a word that has been misused and put out of context. Submission doesn't mean being someone's slave. It is a word of authority it means you are under the authority of your husband just the same way we are under the authority of the Lord Jesus Christ. Many women I have heard think of that word as a insult, no it isn't an insult if you understand its meaning in the context of love and by this

I mean the God kind of love and not lust. If you are a wife loved by your husband to the point that he can die for you oh yes that is the love the bible talks about in the book of Ephesians concerning men, they are to love their wives as Christ loved us. So how did Christ love us? He died for us, that is the kind of Love He had for us. So now do you see why it's easy to submit to a man who can put his life in danger to save you? That is what it means, of course it would not work if a woman is beaten and insulted everyday, there would be no submission because there is no love, but where there is love there is submission, in fact it comes on automatically.

1 Corinthians 11:3

But I would have you know, that the head of every man is Christ; and the head of the woman is the man; and the head of Christ is God.

Ephesians 5: 22-24

Wives, submit yourselves unto your own husbands, as unto the Lord. For the

husband is the head of the wife, even as Christ is the head of the church: and he is

the saviour of the body. Therefore as the church is subject unto Christ, so let the wives be to their own husbands in every thing.

Ephesians 5:33
Nevertheless let every one of you in particular so love his wife even as himself; and

the wife see that she reverence her husband.

I like the amplified version for this verse of Ephesians 5:33 it says:

However, let each man of you [without exception] love his wife as [being in a sense] his very own self; and let the wife see that she respects and reverences her husband [that she notices him, regards him, honors him, prefers him, venerates, and esteems him; and that she defers to him, praises him ad loves and admires him exceedingly].

Again I would like to connect this verse with others in I Peter 3:1-6 in the same version of the bible and it says this;
In like manner, you married women, be submissive to your own husbands [subordinate yourselves as being secondary to and dependent on them, and adapt yourselves to them], so that even if any do not obey the

Word [of God], they may be won over not by discussion but by the [godly] lives of their wives.

When the observe the pure and modest way in which you conduct yourselves, together with your reverence [for your husband; you are to feel for him all that reverence includes: to respect, defer to, revere him- honor, esteem, appreciate, prize and in the human sense, to adore him, that is, to admire, praise, be devoted to, deeply love, and enjoy your husband].

Let not yours be the [merely] external adorning with [elaborate] interweaving and knotting of the hair, wearing of jewelry or changes of clothes.

But let it be the inward adorning and beauty of the hidden person of the heart, with the incorruptible and unfading charm of a gentle and peaceful spirit, which [is not anxious of wrought up, but] is very precious in the sight of God.

For it was thus that the pious women of old who hoped in God were [accustomed] to beautify themselves and were submissive to their husbands [adapting themselves to them as themselves secondary and dependent upon them].

It was thus that Sarah obeyed Abraham [following his guidance and acknowledging his headship over her by] calling him lord (master, leader, authority). And you are now her true daughters if you do right and let nothing terrify you [not giving way to hysterical fears or letting anxieties unnerve you].

If you have patiently read all these verses with me then we can now go step by step analyzing what the Lord is telling us here as women and those of us who are wives should do. One thing I would like to bring to your attentions is that the Lord through Paul is not saying that women should not wear make up or have nice hair styles like pleating or braiding hair or weaving or doing anything nice to our hair. He is also not against jewelry or nice clothes what He is against is, doing all this without a heart that is gentle and peaceful, a heart that is not corrupted with issues of outside beauty without the inner beauty of heart. So then a beautiful woman on the outside is not what the Lord is looking for here it's a woman with inner beauty full of the Spirit of God. That is the only way you can be peaceful and gentle because the Holy Spirit is the only one who can produce such fruit from your heart, (Galatians 5:22-23). We as wives are suppose to reverence our own husbands. This is to respect him, to honor him not to insult, I guess this is obvious that honor goes hand in hand with respect remember this is not fear but respect, to appreciate your husband for the effort he is doing to provide for the family both financially and with time and love towards the family, this brings a question to my mind and I would like you as a wife to ask yourself this question; when did I last tell my husband thank you? You may be asking for what, its his responsibility to provide for the home so why thank him? You could be right its his responsibility but its your responsibility too to appreciate him that is what the Lord requires of you as a wife, so thank him for being a father, for being a good husband, for working hard for the family and sacrificing sometimes for the sake of the family, I am sure you as a wife can find many things to be grateful for. That right there could be key to a long lasting and happy family even if it was in the verge of divorce its amazing how appreciating someone can change their attitude and perspective towards a breaking marriage. Did you know that pride can make a marriage come to an end? Yes if there is not spouse that is willing to bend low and accept to be wrong. No one is perfect in a marriage only God is perfect, in that case then we as women should be in the habit of not trying to change your husband but you should change first and then leave the Lord Holy Spirit deal with your husband. We as wives are also suppose to admire our own husbands not a pastor or an actor or some movie star or athlete, we are to praise and admire our own husbands not our friend's husband but our own. This is very important especially nowadays where people are full of ingratitude and self love to the point that they think that there are perfect spouses in this earth that can make a marriage work and make it exciting; no there are no perfect spouses on earth; there is none so you have to make your marriage work you work it for yourself, you are the one to make it exciting not by introducing perversion into your home, you must make a choice to have a happy long lasting marriage and let the Lord Holy Spirit be your guide and helper in your marriage. I remember I had to surrender my marriage to the Lord Holy Spirit 5 years ago and let Him run the show and I would be right behind Him to follow what He tells me and I can testify and say I am enjoying my marriage now more and more its getting more exciting, I love it but it was not so when I got married 7 years ago I had to make the choice and you also have to make your own if you are married.

Another thing the Word tells us to do is to be devoted to our husbands, this means your husband can never be the point of discussion in the salon or in your family get together, you are devoted to serving him with love and confidentiality, of course you can share your problems if you have with trusting friends or pastor or parents but not with everyone, I hope you get what I mean. The last questions I would want you to ask yourself as a wife is how deep do you love your husband? Do you enjoy having him? How is your sex life? Do you desire your own husband? Do you communicate all the time whether things are good or bad?

These are some of the questions if you answer no to can tell you that you are not having a healthy marriage and so you can address the issues and invite the Lord to help you and give you solutions to the problems you have, trust me He will. And remember God loves you and wants your marriage to be the best so ask Him anything you do not understand and He will direct your path.

My prayer for all married women that read this book is that, the Lord Holy Spirit will teach you and direct you in your marriages as you meditate on the verses above and give you a rhema word for your situation in your marriage so that you can enjoy, desire, praise, honor, respect, love and submit to your own husband.

1 Corinthians 7:14

For the Christian wife brings holiness to her marriage, and the Christian husband brings holiness to his marriage. Otherwise, your children would not have a godly influence, but now they are set apart for him.

THE PRINCIPAL THING

In verse 7 of proverbs chapter 4 sums it all up and says this; *wisdom is the principal thing*

Isn't Christ Jesus the principal thing in life? Yes He is the main reason for living; He is life and He gives us life in abundance.

Proverbs 1:7 (AMP)
The reverent and worshipful fear of the Lord is the beginning and the principal and choice part of knowledge [its starting point and its essence]: but fools despise skillful and goldly Wisdom, instruction and discipline.

And so if you have Christ living in you then the spirit of the Lord who in Isaiah 11:2 tells us that He is the spirit of the fear of the Lord, will help you walk in the fear of the Lord and teach you how to reverentially fear and worship the Lord. I think this is the reason we have very few scriptures in the new covenant talking about walking in the fear of the Lord let me explain it this way;

FEAR OF THE LORD= BEGINNING OF WISDOM = CHRIST JESUS

So we can conclude and say then that if you are born again, that is redeemed by our Lord Jesus Christ, filled with the Lord

Holy Spirit then you can walk in the fear of the Lord and become the ideal woman that God created you to be.

GIRL TALK

I always like looking back in my life and sort of analyze the quality of life I had and what I have now. I don't know if you do that but in case you do not, try one day and sit down and just look back at your life and ask yourself this question just this one only; has my life been reflecting Christ? If your answer is yes then keep on doing and adding more value to your life for Him but if your answer is no then there is hope and it's never too late to turn back to the arms of a loving Father and Savior.

I hope this testimony of my life will encourage you to seek God with all your heart and you will find out that life is worth living and you are worth living in this planet for Christ, read this please would you?

I am a 32 year old Kenyan woman born in a family of 9 children I am the last born of these and at the tender age of 19 my mother died, this was like the worst day of my life and in my little brain I thought my life is finished and doomed. I was born in a Christian family but did not have a personal relationship with our Lord Jesus Christ and so I was very bitter with God because I thought He let my mother die and yet He could have done something, oh how wrong I was. By the way my mother died of diabetes and it was because of poverty and lack of knowledge that was in my family then that killed her not God, God is a good God and He never left me even after my mum died. Because is this anger in me I did not pray to the Lord for a whole year and didn't even bother to read the bible. I thank God for His grace, mercy and love that endures for ever because He loved me even when I was angry and running away from Him.

So to make this testimony short I went to live with one of my relatives where I got so depressed and over weight. Words like "you will never amount to anything" were said other words like "your father is wasting money on you and you cannot make good grades in the university" were said about me and so many others that I wouldn't like to mention here but by the grace of God I fell back onto His loving arms again through watching Trinity Broadcasting Network (TBN) which is a Christian TV channel and there I got so much hope that my life would one day change. At the time I was doing my bachelors degree in a local university and I was not making good grades and that added to my frustrations. I also got married to my husband when I was in my third year in the university and that really upset my relatives but I didn't know that my marriage was a turning point for me.

Well when I got married and later finished my degree we moved cities I became a house wife and this lead even to deeper depression because of the bitter words I would hear from my relatives in fact there was a day I called my uncle and he reminded me of the miserable life my mother used to live and told me that I was choosing the same path. I was really hurt by the statement but I was determined to prove them wrong that I was worth something I was a child of God and not what they thought I was. I was overweight to the point that I looked like a puffed up balloon I was weighing almost 100 KG! that is over 200 pounds and this made me have a very low self esteem and have thoughts of worthlessness but the Lord Jesus through reading His word and doing the Word not just listening, has changed my life. I am now a different person the Lord blessed me and I got my baby boy and the amazing thing was through all this my husband was always loving and encouraging me. I call him a man of God because the Lord used him to get the pearl out of a broken and marred girl. So while I was at home and going through all the ridicule from friends and relatives of how dam I was to be sitting in the house as a graduate instead of looking for a job and work, the Lord Holy Spirit started teaching me different truths in the bible which lead to the writing of this book and others to come. I am now weighing less and less because I have learnt how to take care of the Lord's temple by exercising and eating healthy food. I am happy to be bringing up my son and being there for him all the time when he needs me. I am now living a fulfilled and content life. You see my friend, sometimes you go through hard times in your life but that doesn't mean that it is the end of the road for you, your testimony may be more dramatic than mine but hard times come to shape your destiny I heard someone say that the bigger your Goliath the bigger your destiny just like King David, there is hope in Christ Jesus so I just want to encourage you to take up your cross and follow Christ, surrender totally to Him read the Word of God and do what is says and see how He can get pure gold from miry clay, that is what He did for me and He is no respecter of persons. He will do it for you if you trust Him and be a doer of His Word.

THIS IS WHO YOU ARE IN CHRIST JESUS

I would like to share these scriptures with you my friend so that you can know who you are in Christ the Son of God. Knowing who you are in Christ will erase everything anyone ever told you about yourself including yourself! If you have a low self esteem I would encourage you to read these scriptures daily and meditate on them each time a worthless thought comes your way speak these scriptures aloud to yourself and let the devil hear them too the bible tells us to resist the devil and he will flee.

- ❖ In Christ you are more than a conqueror
  Romans 8:37
  Nay, in all these things we are more than conquerors through him that loved us.
- ❖ In Christ you have greater power in you than the one in this world-
  1 John 4:4
  Ye are of God, little children, and have overcome them: because greater is he that is in you, than he that is in the world.
- ❖ In Christ you are a child of God-
  John 1:12

But to all who believed him and accepted him, he gave the right to become children of God.

- ❖ In Christ you are righteous which means you are in right standing with God-

Romans 3:22

Even the righteousness of God which is by faith of Jesus Christ unto all and upon all them that believe: for there is no difference:

Philippians 3:9

And be found in him, not having mine own righteousness, which is of the law, but that which is through the faith of Christ, the righteousness which is of God by faith:

- ❖ In Christ you are sealed with the Lord Holy Spirit -

Ephesians 1:13

In whom ye also trusted, after that ye heard the word of truth, the gospel of your salvation: in whom also after that ye believed, ye were sealed with that holy Spirit of promise,

Ephesians 4:30

And grieve not the holy Spirit of God, whereby ye are sealed unto the day of redemption.

- ❖ In Christ you are not condemned-

Romans 8:1

There is therefore now no condemnation to them which are in Christ Jesus, who walk not after the flesh, but after the Spirit.

- ❖ In Christ you are a new creature and so the old you is no longer there you are born again that means you are a new person in Christ. The old is gone and the new has come.-

2 Corinthians 5:17

Therefore if any man be in Christ, he is a new creature: old things are passed away; behold, all things are become new.

- ❖ In Christ you are healed because by His stripes we were healed, you can now enjoy divine health.

Isaiah 53:5

But he was wounded for our transgressions, he was bruised for our iniquities: the chastisement of our peace was upon him; and with his stripes we are healed.

1 Peter 2:24

Who his own self bare our sins in his own body on the tree, that we, being dead to sins, should live unto righteousness: by whose stripes ye were healed.

- ❖ In Christ you have overcome the world-

    1 John 5:4

    For whatsoever is born of God overcometh the world: and this is the victory that overcometh the world, even our faith.

- ❖ In Christ you are born of God that means the Living God of Israel is your father

    1 John 5:1

    Whosoever believeth that Jesus is the Christ is born of God: and every one that loveth him that begat loveth him also that is begotten of him.

- ❖ In Christ the devil cannot touch you, hallelujah!

    1 John 5:18

    We know that whosoever is born of God sinneth not; but he that is begotten of God keepeth himself, and that wicked one toucheth him not.

- ❖ In Christ you can do all things because He is there to strengthen you

    Philippians 4:13

I can do all things through Christ which strengtheneth me.

- ❖ In Christ your prayers are answered
  2 Corinthians 1:20
  For all the promises of God in him are yea, and in him Amen, unto the glory of God by us.

GOD BLESS YOU AND ALL YOU ENDEVOUR TO DO IN YOUR LIFE IN CHRIST JESUS. I PRAY THAT THIS BOOK HAS BEEN A BLESSING TO YOU. I PRAY IN THE NAME OF JESUS THAT YOU WILL BE ALL HE DESIGNED YOU TO BE AND THAT YOU WILL FULFILL THE PURPOSE OF GOD IN YOUR LIFE. I LOVE YOU WITH THE LOVE OF CHRIST JESUS.